EVALUATION IN ACTION

Theory and Practice for Effective Evaluation

Gillian Squirrell

Russell House Publishing

First published in 2012 by:
Russell House Publishing Ltd.
58 Broad Street
Lyme Regis
Dorset DT7 3QF

Tel: 01297-443948
Fax: 01297-442722
e-mail: help@russellhouse.co.uk
www.russellhouse.co.uk

Supporting resources, such as checklists, assessment exercises, additional tools for participatory evaluation and discussion papers can be downloaded from www.e2rc.net.

British Library Cataloguing-in-publication Data:
A catalogue record for this book is available from the British Library.

ISBN: 978-1-905541-76-8

Typeset by TW Typesetting, Plymouth, Devon

Printed by IQ Laser Press, Aldershot

About Russell House Publishing

Russell House Publishing aims to publish innovative and valuable materials to help managers, practitioners, trainers, educators and students.

Our full catalogue covers: families, children and young people; engagement and inclusion; drink, drugs and mental health; textbooks in youth work and social work; workforce development.

Full details can be found at www.russellhouse.co.uk and we are pleased to send out information to you by post. Our contact details are on this page.

We are always keen to receive feedback on publications and new ideas for future projects.

Contents

Prologue

The value that a person, an organisation, a community or society places on one thing as opposed to another has come to matter more profoundly than ever in this time of difficult and complex political, economic and moral decision-making during which this book is being published. The ideas and practices explored in this book are often the means used by those making decisions about where scarce money is to be spent for measuring and establishing this value.

Evaluation is a powerful tool: one that may be used to endorse actions and choices that may leave us stuck with existing ways of doing things; or one that may be used to stimulate change and creation. Evaluation is more than a tool, a blunt instrument. There are many ways of thinking about, approaching and undertaking evaluation that can be creative, enabling, inclusive and socially innovative.

A tool of the powerful to preserve the status quo? Or an opportunity for new voices to enable creativity and change? What evaluation becomes in any of our hands is a matter of choice. This book helps make that choice an informed one. It has been written to support and extend professional community practice, to provoke reflection and encourage critical thinking.

Who this book is for

There are many books about evaluation. Some are how-to manuals, others more esoteric drill-downs into particular methodological concerns. *Evaluation in Action* is neither. It seeks to:

- give you the opportunity to understand a range of different approaches to framing and undertaking an evaluation
- help you explore a range of evaluation designs and tools to do the work, some of which are more inclusive, some less so
- encourage you to think how to select the right tools
- encourage you to think about how to work with the learning from an evaluation to stimulate project and organisational changes
- help you to think about some of the methodologies of evaluation, and how to combine them with practice

If you are an experienced evaluator, you will find some stimulating and fresh approaches here. You will be encouraged to reflect on your practice, how you design evaluations, and how you develop contracts to undertake them for others. You will be challenged to think about some aspects of evaluation unfamiliar to you, and feel supported, as aspects of evaluation such as field relationships and the boundaries to an evaluation are explored.

If you are new to evaluation, perhaps not even completely sure what it might be, for example as a new employee, volunteer, intern or student, *Evaluation in Action* has been written with you also in mind. The book is intended to be accessible, to be informative and to offer explanations about some of the terminology which may seem confusing. It puts an evaluation together step-by-step, highlighting many of the points at which choices have to be made, and the implications of those choices. It offers many practical ideas.

If you are commissioning evaluations, this book should help you, when working through the various phases; from discussion about purpose, to commissioning an evaluation, to knowing how to make use of it.

This book is intended to be useful to a broad audience:

- **The commissioner of evaluations**: how can you be sure you are asking for the most appropriate work?
- **The evaluator**: are you aware of different ways of doing evaluation, and how other people may think about each of them?
- **People coming into contact with evaluation**, as stakeholders. Do you want to get involved, or let others make value judgments for you? How might you become involved? Knowing how to do, read, comment on and play a part in evaluations is important
- **Organisations wanting to develop an evaluation strategy**: this book gives a good overview of the role of evaluation and the various ethical and political choices to be made. It helps organisations think about how to learn from an evaluation
- **Students**, lecturers and researchers

Does evaluation matter?

We live in times where much is questioned; and many people expect to comment on what goes on, locally and nationally, in government and at work, in education and health care and community settings.

With such high expectations about involving people, obtaining value for money, and achieving the best possible results, evaluation has become a key tool in decision-making. It is important that as citizens, we understand that so much about evaluation is political. It is not something that is value-free; nothing is. We need to understand how evaluations are undertaken and, in turn, how to evaluate them.

Evaluation may seem dull, pointless and a waste of money. But, like democracy, if you don't take part in a critical and thoughtful engagement with the world around you, when an evaluation gives you that chance at some level, you are handing over power and authority to those that do.

Its all about people; and it gets emotional

Even when they focus on getting best value for money, many evaluations are about people. Who should the money be spent on? And on whom should it not? An evaluation can shake up how societies, organisations and projects are run; or it can preserve the status quo. It will always involve making choices.

The next section of this book starts out with a provocative statement that evaluation can be frightening. This might be because someone is frightened of the work involved, and have no experience of how to do it. Or it might be because your project is to be evaluated by someone else: will the evaluation recommend that you get fresh resources, and continue, or be shut down? This book sets such fears on their head. With knowledge of what is possible, and what certain decisions might mean, evaluation can be a powerful way of supporting democratic developments, innovations and creativity.

Helpful resources

An associated book, *Engagement in Practice* has been written, like this book, to support and extend professional and community practice, to provoke reflection and to encourage critical thinking.

The two books can be read without reference to each other. But taken together, they stimulate thought and action as to how any individual, organisation or community can play a full part in the systems of citizen, consumer and client involvement that have been developing in recent decades, and which continue to develop.

Engagement in Practice and *Evaluation in Action* both have supporting resources, such as checklists, assessment exercises, additional tools for participatory evaluation and discussion papers. These can be found at http://www. e2rc.net. They are referenced in the main text or the notes at the end of each chapter.

This book

Evaluation in Action offers the reader a smorgasbord of approaches, issues and positions for thinking about, and undertaking, evaluation. It encourages you to find and develop new ways of working. There is no reason to become stuck in methodological or evaluation design ruts.

The book may be enough for you for now, but throughout there are pointers to other resources and lines of enquiry for your developing practice.

About the Author

Dr Gillian Squirrell describes her career as social sciences in action. With an academic background in social sciences and management she has worked for over 20 years in research evaluation, training, organisational development and as a social entrepreneur. She has worked in and been contracted to universities, research and development institutes, the public sector and non-profits.

She founded and was the CEO of a residential, learning and training project for offenders and substance misusers for 10 years.

She has undertaken many national evaluations of social policy and programme interventions, run national consultations and researched and trained extensively in areas of programme development, evaluation, engagement and the interplay of research, policy and practice development.

As an organisational consultant and manager she has been actively engaged in working with change in organisations and mediating the various challenges that changes to programme expectations and budgets can present. She works extensively with action research and action learning and systems theory.

She is currently researching and developing a new vocationally geared social enterprise programme for excluded adults. More information about the author can be found at www.gilliansquirrell.net.

There was high praise for Gillian Squirrell's earlier Russell House publications. The three bestselling training manuals – *Becoming an Effective Trainer* (1998) and *Developing Life Skills* (1998) and *Developing Social Skills* (1999) – were acclaimed in many published reviews, and remain both in print and in widespread use. *Becoming an Effective Trainer* was described as 'Particularly valuable . . . It is presented accessibly and balances theory and practice'. *Community Care*. 'An ongoing source of reference and help.' *Youthwork*. 'Promotes all the right messages.' www.trainingzone.co.uk.

Introduction

The history of evaluation is one of fear.

Walker et al., 2000[1]

This is a provocative statement and one to be explored and challenged in this introduction as some of the more vibrant and socially inclusive aspects of evaluation as a discipline are revealed. This Introduction:

- outlines the intentions of this book
- explores chapter contents
- outlines some developments of the short history of evaluation
- explores some features and themes of evaluation that thread through the book

The intentions of this book

Evaluation, a word and an activity that can drive some people to defensiveness and which others use to push them there because, while the outputs of evaluation do nothing in their own right, they can be used as justification for serious actions: programme expansions, or closures; employing more staff, or closing lines of provision.

To other people, evaluation can seem dull: a burdensome requirement of a funding bid, or an additional time-consuming chore imposed on the already hard-pressed. For them, when asked about evaluation, what springs to mind is dreariness: a series of questionnaire-style surveys assessing the impact of an intervention and resulting in reports of horrific detail offering minute statistical significances.

While to others, evaluation represents a crashing waste of resources, stating nothing but the obvious but dressed up in jargon. In this vision, an army of evaluators proclaiming their 'mantra of modernity' roam the private and public sectors, inhabiting 'every facet of life from agriculture to zymurgy'. They descend in the huge numbers on managers and administrators, in the UK as elsewhere, claiming that evaluation 'confers the power to make decisions'.[2]

Yet evaluation is something most people engage in most of the time. It is the critical and thoughtful engagement with the world around us. This book is not going to undersell the knowledge and skill involved in evaluation, nor suggest that it is something everyone can or wants to do. But it does intend to take some of the fear out of evaluation, and to counteract any sense that it is a dull pursuit. It shows how:

- it is helpful to find hard evidence of the original intentions behind an intervention, and what actually happened in its delivery
- engaging in evaluative thinking can develop transferable skills
- evaluation helps us make better-informed decisions
- evaluation can be a way to understand what works, and what does not
- evaluation can be a way to think about change, and what change is needed

Combining some of the theory of evaluation with discussion about its practice, the book is intended to be useful to a broad audience. *Evaluation in Action* offers a discussion of purposes and methodologies of evaluation and is designed to encourage wider thinking about approaches to evaluation.

Evaluation does not have to involve people being treated as the objects of someone else's quasi experiment, nor does it have to exist solely as a bureaucratic imposition. This book explores the ways some types of evaluation can support participation and the development of voice amongst people who have been rendered more marginal in society. It shows how evaluation can be used to support organisational learning, and how a form of evaluation, developmental evaluation, can work at the forefront of social innovation, in real time, with social entrepreneurs informing their decision-making as they creatively tackle complex social issues.

The content of this book

Given the wide claims about it, evaluation can feel confusing. What is it? What should it set out to do? What is its sphere of operation? Is it a discipline in its own right or a sub-branch of the social sciences? Why is there so much of it? How should it be defined? What does it mean to be formative? How can evaluations be inclusive? These are some of the many questions this book addresses.

Setting out to broaden perceptions about the possibilities for evaluation, Chapter 1 explores four reasons for evaluation, from generating knowledge through to supporting innovative programmes, and four approaches to evaluation including Fourth Generation[3] and democratic evaluation.

Chapter 2 outlines some frameworks for programme development and evaluative work including logic models and theories of change.

Chapter 3 discusses organisational learning, and explores the role that evaluations may play in both learning and change.

Chapters 4 to 6 work through a range of important and practical issues: the politics of evaluation and its uses; ethical issues in undertaking evaluations; and the process of contracting an evaluation. It suggests that failure to put time into the contract stage is to invite difficulties into the evaluative relationship.

Chapters 7 to 10 cover the stages from design through to working with the report. Particular attention is given to the discussion of the role of stakeholders, and showing how evaluations may be used to shore up an existing power base, or how they may be crafted and undertaken in ways to challenge the *status quo*.

This introduction opened with statements about some of the more negative ways in which evaluation may be perceived, and throughout the book there is full acknowledgement of the very human dimensions of the evaluative relationship. The final chapter explores the management of feelings in these relationships and the role of the evaluator.

Evaluation in Action offers the reader a range of approaches, issues and positions for conceptualising and undertaking evaluation. It encourages the view that evaluation is unfailingly interesting. For example, the way it contributes to democratic practice and innovation. At a pragmatic level, it presents complex challenges of how best to combine purpose with appropriate research questions, constituencies of stakeholders and the inevitable management of constraints such as budget and commissioners' reporting deadlines. Evaluations can contribute to theory building or knowledge generation. There is much to take from the smorgasbord offered in this book, and very little reason to get stuck in methodological or design ruts.

The rest of this Introduction helps us locate, and take steps towards defining, evaluation. It then highlights some of its major features, and closes with an overview of themes that run throughout the book.

Locating evaluation: a historical note

Evaluation is comparatively new compared with other traditions within the sciences and social sciences. Patton, a seminal figure in evaulation's development, writes of it becoming a distinctive field within the social sciences only in the 1960s. There remain multiple tensions around it. Is it a discipline in its own right? Is it a branch of applied social sciences? What is the relationship of evaluation to research? What is its relationship to theory?

Evaluation has grown exponentially over the past 50 years; in the prevalence of its use and the number approaches. Pawson and Tilley describe it as a 'vast, lumbering, overgrown adolescent' with the problems associated with adolescence. 'It does not know quite where it is going and it is prone to bouts of despair'.[4] In 2000 Robson[5] described it as not quite yet 'fully professionalised'.

Evaluation is found in huge national programmes and in small locally based non-profit organisations. In thinking about evaluation design there are battles for some between the scientific approaches of positivism and post-positivist or constructionist paradigms. In simple terms, is it a search for 'truth', or are there multiple truths? These battles have real bite in the world of evaluation, perhaps because the stakes are high, ranging from the validation of resource expenditure to the issuing of marching orders for a programme. Much of contemporary life is managed through reviews, appraisals, audits, performance management, performance indicators and evaluation. How have we reached this point of evaluation undergirding managerialism?

The next few pages explore how the landscape of evaluation has come to be this way. This outline history lays out some of the bigger methodological issues and questions of use. It is not a clear history, with each type of evaluation tied to a specific timeline; after its comparatively simple beginnings, the evaluation story began its adolescent sprawl. It includes the emergence of different methodologies and approaches, which are not tied into single decades, but which evolve, and jostle for position over longer periods of time on the menu of evaluation options. There are surges of emphasis and different rationales for use, again, not always tied to particular decades. This account provides an overview of the historical development of ideas, and provides a 'big picture' context, before some of the ideas are discussed in more detail in later chapters.

1940s: positivism, experimental and quasi-experimental models

The early days of evaluative work, from the 1940s, the First, Second and Third Generations of evaluation, were based on an understanding of enquiry based on positivism. The intentions were measurement of the extent to which an intervention worked (First Generation, for example IQ measurement) description of what was working (Second Generation) and judgment about the nature of the intervention (Third Generation).

The work was based on testing people who had experienced an intervention and comparing them with a control group.[6] The evaluator approximated to a natural scientist, whose role in the evaluation was considered neutral as they worked alongside those who devised and managed the programmes under review, and who undertook evaluations on groups of evaluands.[7] The power dynamic in this relationship was not explored because for most it was not considered appropriate. The assumption that the programme under scrutiny was the right programme was likewise not at issue.

1960s: evaluation comes of age

Evaluations continued in this vein, until in the 1960s when they came of age with the first great waves of evaluation in the US Great Society social welfare and reform programmes. With these huge programmes came huge costs, and evaluation had the role of assessing what was happening in order to inform decisions about resource management. It was intended that social policy be grounded within evaluation research.

These evaluations were based on the logic of natural science experiments and the theory of causation. This classic experimental design is explored further in Chapter 1. Evaluation methodology was based on trying to explain the impact of an intervention, the basic design being that of the experimental group, receiving the intervention, and a similar group, a control group, which does not. The model described as OXO works as follows:

	Pre-test or pre-intervention	Treatment or intervention	Post-test or post-intervention
Experimental group	O	X	O
Control group	O		O

Diagram 1: The OXO Model

While these assumptions and form of research may work well in a laboratory it is harder in the social world to infer causation. As many variables as possible need to be excluded from the situation, so that there can be relative certainty of a causal link.

During the late 1960s and 1970s there was significant social experimentation with large-scale welfare and social programmes in educational and social policy contexts, trying to generate what were considered desirable social improvements by policy makers. The experimenting society was expensive and there was a need to understand in policy terms what worked. This debate rumbled on through the next 30 years.

It became clear that the simple OXO approach did not answer all the questions, and that there may be data both in support of an intervention and against an intervention, based on particular target groups and on context. A more nuanced approach than the experimental or quasi-experimental approaches could offer was required.

Other approaches to evaluation were developed in order to address issues about which interventions were working, so as to inform the development of social policy. Policymaking was demanding information; the history of evaluation continued with a role to play in policy development and the management of resource expenditure. Evaluators saw a need to factor in those very variables that the quasi-experimentalists had tried to factor out: the political and social contexts in which interventions were taking place.

While this Introduction moves on to explore other forms of evaluation methodology, it is important to appreciate that we are just parting from experimental or positivist methodology. These approaches continue to thrive in parallel to other and newer methodologies. It remains a very dominant paradigm within evaluation research; it is just that other contenders join the race.

The 1980s

Rather than see an intervention as something that could be isolated from its social context and from political choices, and be put under the microscope for pre-and post-test review, the social, political and contextual elements were factored in to some methodologies in evaluation research.

Constructivism, an understanding in the social sciences that people create multiple interpretations of the same thing and that people experience multiple realities in parallel, came to inform some of the ways in which researchers began to think about evaluation. Data collection moved beyond the experimental subjects to a far wider group of people involved in the intervention. Their very differing interpretations and understandings of what was happening were valued as data.

One particular development of the constructivist approach was that of Fourth Generation evaluation. Here, working to a protocol, the views of many types of stakeholders in an intervention were sought. The circle of the enquiry was spread beyond the experimental subjects of positivist approaches to a far wider group of people involved in the intervention. The stakeholders moved from being subjects of an evaluation to collaborators. In this way the research moved from the experimenter reporting on causal links to being the go-between between various stakeholders to discover a more consensual view of the intervention and its impacts. In the language of Fourth Generation evaluation this is the 'hermeneutic dialogue circle'.

The importance of realities being understood as constructions meant that the researcher had to be seen as part of the process of constructing, rather than as being something outside the process. Moreover, the researcher was seen as part of the context of what was being researched. This meant that those evaluations which were developed using constructivist or Fourth Generation paradigms did not claim to be generalisable to other contexts.

However, there is more to reality than just individuals' perceptions. Social institutions and structures exert influence in an intervention. Evaluation can sometimes be criticised for its failure to take into account the different power positions of people involved, both in decision-making and in experiencing an intervention. Politics and power relationships in evaluation are discussed at greater length, later in this introduction and in Chapter 5.

Alongside a development of a pluralism of methods ran discussions about why evaluations were being undertaken. The 1980s for example saw the rise of pragmatism or utilisation-focused evaluation. Utilisation-focused evaluation is both a statement about the reason for evaluation and an approach to working to secure this. The intention was that the data be used in some way. Utilisation-focused evaluation suggested, if there was no specification of methodology from those commissioning the work, then the evaluator should use their discretion to collect the data in any ways which would bring issues to the surface, and so make the findings as pertinent and as informative for use as possible.

The 1990s

The developments of the next decade saw greater acceptance of more pluralist approaches to evaluation, specifically the attempt to combine breadth and depth. One such example was theory-driven evaluation; but there were problems in trying to define what was theory, and in making this into something more than another experimentalist approach, with a hunt for the effectiveness of theory built in, while ignoring context. Theory based evaluation is explored in Chapters 1 and 2.

Chapter 1 also outlines Realist Evaluation, which has developed a protocol for ways to pick apart an intervention so as to understand better what elements work, for which groups and in which contexts. As a methodology it breaks with the dominance of quantitative methods.

The development of many more approaches, and their acceptance, has been described by Patton as giving rise to a menu of options for evaluators and commissioners. While methodologically evaluators had to align with a positivist or post-positivist approach, there were no rules about the combination of methods which were informed by these two paradigms. In fact adopting a mixed methods approach was seen as likely to strengthen the quality of the data. These ideas represented a significant development from the early days of quasi-experimental evaluations.

There were further new approaches in the 2000s, with for example developmental evaluation gaining in strength at the start of the second decade of the century. This is explored in Chapters 1 and 2.

The 1990s and 2000s: the rise of the trinity of outcome monitoring, evaluation and quality assurance

Meanwhile, there has been continued political commitment to the value and the uses of evaluation in decision-making.

Evaluation had become so much a part of reviewing social and welfare programmes, and scaled-down programmes, that the mid 1990s saw the national evaluation societies founded in UK, US and Australia, evaluation journals published, and cycles of international conferences on evaluation get underway. Within various arenas of social policy and practice development there was systematic development of programmes based on a What Works approach and, in some instances, the sharing of evaluative findings internationally. For example, Scotland, England and parts of the US shared evaluation-based correctional programmes for various groups of offenders in prison.

These decades saw a triumph of quality assurance and quality control movements; management was undergirded by a drive to performance improvement and the institution of excellence-based models for the provision of services and products. Responsibility for ensuring the quality of provision was pushed down the management line to front-line staff, and performance was measured according to targets and results. Evaluation had a part to play in this.

> *Evaluation techniques are essential tools of management practice today. No professional can afford not to take an analytic approach to the job to be done. Evaluation is the first step towards improving your own performance and the performance of others – the precursor to maximising effectiveness, the mechanism for minimising ineffectiveness.*
>
> Breakwell, 1995[8]

Given these sentiments it is easy to understand why evaluation could be perceived in instrumental and management terms as being about decision-making based on efficiencies, with perhaps less regard for nuanced understandings of the intervention. Evaluation could be seen as about rubber-stamping management decisions. Breakwell outlines three purposes for evaluation: validation, improvement and condemnation. She links these to the phases of the life cycle of an intervention; validation at start-up to prove the intervention is a good idea; improvement once it is in full flow; and by the final stage, the primary reason for evaluation will be 'condemnation' and service close down. This is a management based set of reasons for decision-making, perhaps based on funding availability and not on perceived need. Breakwell does argue that managers do need better understanding of evaluation, to stop it being used for nefarious organisational purposes. This is, however, a very managerialist take on the role of evaluation.

The 2000s and the rise of evidence-based practice

Alongside the links between evaluation and performance management, ran the movement for evidence-based practice. This underscored the need for evaluation as a research tool to support policy developments and expenditure.

In evidence-based practice evaluation is 'seen as a way of investigating what works best', with the purpose of basing future policy and practice upon the results of the investigation. Blunkett[9] (2000) emphasised the importance of Government policies to be underpinned by good research; and that innovations in policy and practice need to be piloted and tested.

Much of the evidence-based practice movement began in health and has moved to other areas of professional practice. Proponents see evidence-based practice as:

- showing whether or not initiatives will be successful and, depending on the spread of pilot work, successful under a variety of conditions
- enabling the testing of new ideas in a transparent and open way before adoption, therefore supporting transparency of decision-making in policy adoption and government
- supporting the choice of developments which are efficient and which do not waste public resources
- selecting programmes which are proven to deliver value for money
- playing a role in needs analysis to show gaps in services

The era of evidence-based practice ushered in new ways to undertake professional development. There was an emphasis on reflection, on learning-based practice and development of in-house and self-evaluation. Project managers and front-line staff were expected to monitor outputs and outcomes against pre-set targets to demonstrate progress, and to evaluate the effectiveness of programmes. Evaluation became part of process management and of learning why targets were realised, or not.

Alongside this rise of evidence-based practice was the development of partnership working and working across organisational boundaries. This required increasing work-place reflection and a focus on process. Evaluation was an in-built element of these partnership processes and an indication of the extent to which partnership working could contribute to enhanced and effective service delivery.

Where we are now

The preceding pages have outlined something of the history of the evolution of evaluation from its early decades of fairly straight-forward measuring and judging interventions of an experimental approach, through its use in measuring outcomes and for management decisions to the rise of evidence-based practice and helping to shape policy, and so channel financial resources.

Recent decades have seen a development of methodologies, as awareness of the importance of power, politics and uses of evaluation have come to be appreciated. This forces choices on evaluators and commissioners to work with a menu of options, and brings the roles played by evaluators, and those who are involved in the intervention, under scrutiny. The links between evaluation and social policy development, evaluation and resource use, and evaluation and management decisions have been tabled. These threads are taken up in the remainder of the book.

It is clear, however, why Pawson and Tilley described evaluation as an overgrown adolescent with a number of uncertainties about identity and direction. To add a new metaphor, evaluation is expected to play handmaiden in a number of situations, and to fulfil a number of roles.

So far no definition of evaluation has been offered. The next section rather than offer a definition, suggests a number of defining features.

Features of evaluation

'All evaluations are a combination of the social, political and technical'.[10] This is a statement which would be hard to argue with.

Evaluations are social because:

- there is a range of interpersonal relationships involved in the evaluation involving the researcher and the various stakeholders, amongst the stakeholders themselves, and the balance of power between them
- they are about the social world, the perception of social realities and competing needs

Evaluations are political because:

- the evaluation may be informing decisions about an intervention, the use of resources or the development of a programme
- the roles and status of the various stakeholders and the ways these are used, the position of the commissioner, the design and undertaking of the evaluation, and the way the role of the evaluator is constructed and played can all be political
- the findings can be politically contentious or used to political ends

Evaluations are technical because:

- there is a need to adopt a methodology and to adhere to a coherent design for the evaluation
- there are ways in which data need to be collected and analysed in order for there to be trust in the integrity and comprehensiveness of the findings
- with such a large menu of options for ways of working, complex decisions have to be taken to match design with purpose, based on detailed understanding of different methodologies, for example participatory evaluation, which can develop new ways of working to better meet the demands of different contexts and of various stakeholders' needs
- outputs might include ways to undertake capacity building for individuals and communities

The following are some common features of evaluations; their emphasis may vary depending on approach and purpose.

Evaluations are *tied to social worlds*. They may try to illuminate a social world a little more and generate theory or contribute to knowledge, or they may be concerned with something more pragmatic like the efficacy of a programme. Evaluations are applications of social science. Their links to the world mean they have to *work with constraints* and within timeframes; they are mostly commissioned and have to take account of *a purpose beyond themselves*. Evaluations are mostly intended to *be used*, and so should conform to that purpose in the types of reporting and recommendations they make.

Evaluations *collect and weigh data*. Evaluation is about valuing and making *judgments* about something: an intervention, a plan or proposal. It is about assessing needs and making a value judgment of those needs or a judgment of an innovation in the making. How and why the judgment is undertaken is important. This shades into the politics and power that lie behind the process of commissioning an evaluation. They make judgments about evidence. *They do not make decisions*, this is the role of those commissioning the work. The role of recommendations is explored in Chapter 10.

Evaluations are often intended to *inform the development of changes*. These changes may be improvements, such as in a formative evaluation of a programme, but they may be an appreciation of changing circumstances. The nature of the understanding of change is important, as is the value base of the evaluation.

Themes within the book

This book explores a number of themes that underpin evaluation. These include:

Values. Values permeate an evaluation at many stages, from the shaping of the research area and questions, through choices about methodology and how to conduct the evaluation, to work with the findings. These decisions are linked to power and to politics as is explored below. Which stakeholder groups will be given priority is a question of values. It is a matter of whose opinions count, and whose interests are considered significant.

Power. There are many ways in which power may manifest. Some can be flagged in questions such as who commissions an evaluation. Does it represent everyone's interests or focus more narrowly? What questioning does the evaluation encourage or allow of existing ways of working? How are the findings from an evaluation used? How widely are the findings from an evaluation shared? Are changes a result of an evaluation? Which interest groups provide data for the evaluation? What decisions are taken about methods used in an evaluation? These types of actions and decisions all make statements about power, and about which groups might be in control.

Power in the social sciences has been tabled as an issue, and challenged, through the work of, for example, feminist researchers. Feminist researchers have drawn into the frame the experiences of women and young women along with those of many other social and cultural groups. These experiences had previously been excluded as they did not fit the theories of dominant groups. In terms of interventions and the development of programmes, where there are groups whose voices are not heard it will affect the effectiveness of the intervention for them and so the overall effectiveness of the intervention. Evaluation methodologies informed by the work of feminist researchers and others concerned with those who are marginalised, have developed young people's participatory evaluation, participatory evaluation, democratic and personalised evaluation. Methodologies and methods are explored in Chapters 1 and 2, and there is discussion about the theme of power throughout the book.

Politics. Evaluations are mostly concerned with interventions, programmes, policy or practice, all of which are reformist in nature. This gives evaluations a reformist nature as well, trying to find other ways to solve or improve social problems or situations. Evaluations are petty political in that they work with solutions which seek to address or improve existing issues. Evaluation research is infrequently undertaken in ways that question the basis of an existing system or the causes of an issue. It rarely engages in blue skies thinking working towards more radical solutions. It rarely questions given political and social situations.

An appreciation of politics is important in thinking about how to make decisions about evaluations. Chapter 1 introduces democratic and personalised evaluation as a methodology that might shift this balance. Chapter 5 focuses on the politics in undertaking evaluations, both for political or policy development ends and as a means of supporting an existing *status quo*. Chapters 7 to 9 explore decision points in designing an evaluation and in selecting a methodology and methods, which may make evaluation participatory. Chapter 9 focuses completely on participatory evaluation as a methodology and the types of methods and processes at play.

Learning. Evaluation is undertaken to discover something, often about what changes or interventions are working or failing to work. This book is based on the value judgement that evaluations should be useful, that there is little value in an evaluation report that is written to sit in a cupboard. There has therefore to be a process of learning from the evaluation and some action taken. The importance of learning and action are explored in Chapter 3.

The human dimensions. These are often missed in discussions of evaluation. Evaluation is frequently presented as dispassionate, objective and therefore honest. The evaluator is somehow not present, more akin to a natural scientist operating some equipment in an unfeeling and unbiased experiment. Throughout the book this image of evaluation is disturbed. There are discussions of emotions, the skills and needs of internal and external evaluators as they face a variety of field issues and decisions. There are discussions of various elements in the possible interactions of evaluator and evaluand, and discussions of evaluations which are co-created and participatory.

This book

The ideas that have been introduced here show that evaluation is used as a powerful tool, and this power is part of the reason why its theories and methods are so contested. It also explains not only why its products may be destructively employed, and its name taken in vain, but also why it can be used creatively, and be inclusive and enabling.

The choice of how it is used is a personal one.

This book fuses the conceptual, and the analytically descriptive, with engagement in practice. It has been written to support and extend practice, provoke reflection and encourage thinking about the potential value of engagement.

The first part explores some conceptual issues about engagement: its purpose, value, role and developments. The second outlines some of the ways in which engagement may be designed, instigated and undertaken.

Endnotes

1. Walker, P. et al. (2000) *Prove It! Measuring the Effect of Neighbourhood Renewal on People*. London, Groundwork, NEF, Barclays Bank.
2. Pawson, R. and Tilley, N. (1997) *Realistic Evaluation*. London, Sage.
3. The Fourth Generation of evaluation (Guba and Lincoln, 1989) is the development of evaluation based on an understanding of constructionism. This is the break with the logic of experimentalism and moves to an appreciation of the pluralism of views of members of society and appreciation that the social world is constructed. This is explored further in Chapter 1.
4. Pawson, R. and Tilley, N. (1997) *Realistic Evaluation*. London, Sage.
5. Robson, C. (2000) *Small Scale Evaluation*. London, Sage.
6. A control group is either based on a person-by-person match with someone having the intervention or more broadly as a matched group having similar features to the group

experiencing the intervention. More about controls, experimental and quasi-experimental approaches is found in Chapter 1.

7. The term for those evaluated. It is a term though which is open to debate for it suggests a very passive role for those engaged in the evaluation relationship. This returns to the discussion of purpose and methodology.

8. Breakwell, G. and Millward, L. (1995) *Basic Evaluation Methods.* Leicester, British Psychological Society.

9. DfEE, (2000) *Connexions the Best Start in Life For Every Young Person.* Sheffield, DfEE.

10. Baker, A. and Sabo, K. (2004) *Guidebook for Non-profit Organisations and their Evaluation Partners.* Brunner Foundation.

1: Defining the Territory of Evaluation

Introduction

This chapter focuses on some reasons for undertaking evaluations and the methodologies that shape very different approaches to evaluation. A single chapter can only be a taster, but one it is hoped that will stimulate the reader's interest to reflect upon the diversity of the conceptualisation of evaluation and its use.

The chapter explores what some may consider the more dominant approach to evaluation, the quasi-experimental paradigm, informed by the natural sciences. While this might colour much thinking about evaluations there are other ways in which evaluation may be approached and used. Evaluation may be used to theory build to support knowledge generation. It may contribute to the informed and real time development of social interventions. Evaluations may seek to build greater democracy in community decision-making.

These differences in purpose and approach pose questions for the role of the evaluator. Is the evaluator an uninvolved, objective expert developing and undertaking an evaluation which leads to a considered judgment on the worth of an intervention? Is the evaluator working alongside stakeholders as a co-creator in the design and development of the evaluation? Are the evaluator's biases and ways of framing the research questions to be considered along with those of various stakeholder groups? The differences in methodology require consideration of the nature of social reality. Are there one or multiple lived realities and are any more important than others?

The chapter outlines some different methodologies and reasons for evaluation. It opens by outlining four different reasons for evaluation, including making judgments about programme impacts and generating knowledge. It then moves to explore several other methodologies which underpin very different approaches to evaluation, positivist and constructionist paradigms, democratic evaluation and the theory building of realist evaluations.

The chapter can only work with outlines but does so in order to expand the number of possibilities on a menu of evaluative choices for the reader.

Exploring some reasons for evaluating

This section does not offer an exhaustive list of reasons for evaluation, but it offers four quite different ones and ones which can be related to different stages in the development of social interventions and learning about them.

1. Formative and summative

Formative and summative evaluations are those located within the lifecycle of a programme part way through and at its close respectively. The terminology continues to be used in programme evaluation. Formative evaluations explore progress on the way to realising programme objectives and may be used to make judgments about possible programme improvements. Summative evaluations are concerned with the impacts of a complete programme. In current use these purposes are not tied to any particular methods but there is a need in trying to assess both progress and impact in having some baseline data to see distance travelled and final impacts.

In earlier conceptualisations of programme evaluation there were more definite statements about the role of formative and summative evaluations. Scriven,[1] a seminal figure in evaluation research made the following statement:

> There was a formative or improvement-oriented evaluation, which was geared toward making a programme or other intervention better. This type of evaluation applied to some programmes. The majority of evaluations were summative.

Formative and summative in Scriven's thinking were related because ultimately a formative evaluation leads to summative evaluation, because programmes and interventions would reach a steady state without further changes and they could then be evaluated for their impacts. Within any formative evaluation a number of areas would be identified which would later be re-evaluated in the summative evaluation.

Summative evaluations are judgments about a stable and fixed programme which has come to a close. They are an exploration of the merit or worth of the intervention based on 'efficient goal attainment, replicability, clarity of causal specificity and generalisability' (Patton, 2006).[17]

Patton argued in 1996 that this sharp distinction between formative and summative as the purposes of evaluation had become insufficient as a way of conceptualising evaluation. It was one which was very programme focused and this was no longer, according to Patton, enough. More diversity of purpose and approach was needed as evaluation researchers found other ways to look at social and political worlds. Patton argues for a menu of options:[2]

> . . . the original formative-summative formulation thirty years ago was helpful in evaluation's infancy, but as a maturing field of professional practice, it's time to deal with the complexities of open systems, multiple purposes, and diverse values. Judgment-oriented, comprehensive, and summative evaluation is not the apex or the Holy Grail, it is not all of evaluation, and not all formative evaluations are getting ready for summative evaluation. Evaluation serves other purposes including but not limited the following:
>
> - Generating general knowledge about principles and program effectiveness.
> - Developing programs and organisations.
> - Focusing management efforts.
> - Creating learning organisations.
> - Empowering participants.
> - Directly supporting and enhancing program interventions by fully integrating evaluation into the intervention.
> - Stimulating critical reflection on the path to more enlightening practice.

This list written in 1996 continues to have merit. Patton's critique shifts the focus away from thinking about evaluation in terms of the programme and its performance to locating evaluation within a broader range of uses and communities of interest. These purposes and approaches are explored next.

2. Developmental evaluation: reconceptualising programmes and change

Patton was instrumental in this development in evaluation methodology.[3] Developmental evaluation works with an understanding of organisations and programmes informed by complexity theory, emergence and ambiguity. Developmental evaluation can tolerate the effects of non-linearity. That is, that small actions can create large reactions; and dynamic adaptations, interacting elements and agents within a system can respond and adapt to each other in often quite unpredictable ways. This is the sort of environment which is found in situations where developmental work is in process, where there are social innovations addressing complex problems and mapping out a new territory as they go in order to do so. This type of turbulence happens where the operational environment is dynamic and complex, where participants, interventions, and context are in flux and the pathways for achieving desired outcomes are uncertain. It may be that those who are innovating are not themselves sure of their direction and are watching and adapting to changing circumstances. This is not an environment where there will be any sort of intervention that can be described as in a steady state and where an evaluation can be created according to predefined criteria. This situation requires quite a different form of evaluation.

In these situations social innovators need to be informed about their work, impacts and choices, through reliably collected and robustly analysed data. Developmental evaluation supports reality testing, innovation, and adaptation in these complex dynamic systems where relationships among critical elements are nonlinear and emergent. Evaluation in such environments focuses on continuous and ongoing adaptation, intensive reflective practice, and rapid, real-time feedback.[4] The purpose of developmental evaluation is in helping develop and adapt the intervention. This is quite different from formative programme evaluation which seeks to improve a model which is understood and being operationalised.

Developmental evaluation is very much a form of evaluation, which can be described as evaluation in use. This changes the role of the evaluator from distanced and unconnected, passing an arms length judgment to someone who plays an organisational development role. The evaluator in this form of evaluation is someone able to work with the messiness of reality and who compromises between following precepts of evaluation design based on predictions and static models and the need to work to feed data back for real time developmental decisions. Developmental evaluation creates more of a partnership between evaluator and the social innovator to embed evaluative thinking into the innovator's decision-making processes as part of the ongoing design and implementation initiatives.

Social innovation may not go into a steady state programme even in the longer-term, so developmental evaluation would be an on-going need. In these circumstances change would be an outcome of evaluation but change would be about being responsive to the evolving situation and learning from it, not a statement about the quality of what had preceded it.

3. Utilisation evaluation

Utilisation-focused evaluation is another way to undertake formative evaluation and is evaluation for use. It places the stakeholders or users of the evaluation at its heart, and the evaluator plays a supportive and process focused role as opposed to that of an expert making judgments and suggestions. The evaluator works with the stakeholders to develop an evaluation which supports their needs and interests.

Patton who developed utilisation evaluation[5] distinguishes between utilisation and dissemination. Utilisation is more than disseminating findings it is about making sure that the findings are understandable to a wide range of stakeholders. The findings are intended to be shared between the stakeholders and they should reach their own decisions about what actions to take. Utilisation is the *raison d'être* of an evaluation and it is for the stakeholders to do something about what has been discovered. It may not be adopting the findings or recommendations wholesale, but it is to engage with them and explore what adds value for them.

Having a utilisation-focus injects a real world perspective into the conceptualisation of the evaluation, its design, undertaking and reporting. The evaluator is not there to tell the organisation what to do but to explore and explain what has been found thereby supporting them to take some action.

The utilisation-focused evaluation and supportive role for the evaluator has drawn criticism from some, that this is a form of a pseudo-evaluation. Scriven argued that not to pass judgment and tell an organisation what to do but to let a broad range of stakeholders make their own determination was to fly in the face of the role of evaluator and like the evaluator deciding that 'you want to be a virgin after the orgy but before the Day of Judgment'.[6]

Utilisation evaluation has also been criticised by those more committed to methodological purism for designing and undertaking evaluations that take into account constraints such as budget, timeframe and commissioner's purpose, over the demands of a rigorous purely methodologically informed design. If a policy maker needs some data-informed analysis and recommendations but has a five month window for policy development and a more methodologically driven design suggests 18 months, what is to be done? Utilisation evaluators would prefer that there be policy based on some data and analysis as opposed to working on an evaluation, which would not in any account have been commissioned, which arrived 13 months after the need had passed.

Ultilisation evaluators would undertake an evaluation which explored elements of a programme as opposed to looking at a programme in its entirety. Again this may better serve the needs of those commissioning the work and may generate data and analysis which can be better used than a whole programme evaluation. An example of a focused partial evaluation is offered as a worked example in Chapter 7 on evaluation design.

Ulitilisation-focused evaluations require commitment from the users to make use of the evaluation. The intended users' interests will shape each stage of the evaluation's design, undertaking and reporting. It is important to strategise the evaluation, to continuously think how it will help to build understanding and capacity of the intended users to help inform their decision-making and development. This means the evaluation design is situationally adapted, not drawn from standardised ideas as to how an evaluation would run. The evaluator's role is as a different sort of expert working for those commissioning the work.

Utilisation-focused evaluation emphasises the appropriate involvement of a range of stakeholders, not for form's sake but to actively ensure users' commitment to the work, to shape the work to reflect needs and to develop capacity and learning through the evaluation. Patton[7] argues that findings of evaluations have a relatively short half-life and that 'much of the impact of evaluation comes from the process of engaging in evaluation, not from its findings'.

Chapter 7 on design explores some ways in which stakeholders may be identified, the ways in which practical constraints may be factored in and the importance of the users' clarity of purpose and use for the evaluation needs to be established.

4. Evaluation research: knowledge generation

This is a different form of the utilisation of evaluations: rather than use evaluations within a decision-making process in an instrumental way, evaluations are undertaken as research and the intention is to make use of evaluation outcomes as a contribution to knowledge-building. Evaluations having a conceptual purpose can contribute to better understanding a theory or a particular constituency and their needs. They can be used to test theories and models. They can be used to find ways to better evaluate certain types of programmes and their outcomes. They may be used to explore social science theories in action.

Evaluations may be looked at as single items or may be pulled together as a group to explore patterns and lessons emerging from a number of programmes. The evaluations of these programmes may have a number of common reporting elements.

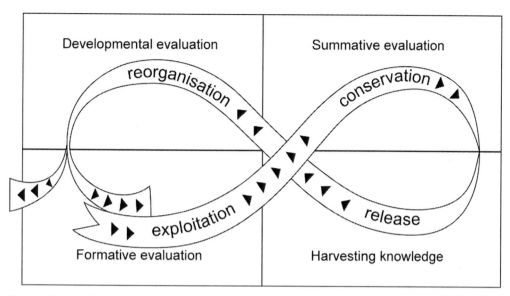

Diagram 2: Panarchy Loop

The emphasis in this type of evaluation is on knowledge development and broader understanding as opposed to a single focus on understanding the programme under review.

Diagram 2 links up these various purposes for evaluations within a systems theory framework. It shows adaptive changes within social systems and is derived from research on adaptive systems within environmental and ecological contexts.[8] The diagram illustrates links between these various types of evaluation and their primary functions and charts the lifecycles of many social interventions and initiatives for which evaluation should, and can, usefully run in parallel.

So adaptive change proceeds through a *forward loop*, with stages of innovation, growth and exploitation, consolidation, predictability and conservation. This is followed by the *back loop* phases of instability, release, collapse, experimentation, novel recombination and reorganisation.

Different approaches to evaluating

Moving from the four reasons outlined above, this section outlines five methodologies: Positivist, Post-Positivistic or Constructivist, Fourth Generation, Realist Evaluation and Democratic Evaluation. Chapter 9 explores another, Participatory Evaluation.

Methodologies may be innovative in their social purpose (Democratic Evaluation) or try to solve methodological problems (Realist Evaluation). Methodologies are not methods, evaluation uses a number of methods found at work in the social sciences, some of which are discussed in Chapter 8. The methodologies outlined here are to demonstrate a breadth of approach to and intentions in undertaking evaluation. The point to embrace here is the importance of thinking through what it is that the evaluation is seeking to discover and select the right methodology to answer the research questions and to suit the situation (Patton, 1982).[9] It is not appropriate to plump for a set of methods and apply them to an evaluation question just because they are what a researcher knows or favours (Clarke, 1999).[10] Evaluation is far more than the application of methods, it has to be driven by reason and methodology.

The first two methodologies discussed are positivism and constructivism. These are perhaps the best-known methodological paradigms, and people have a clear sense of there being a tension between them, failing to appreciate how they might be combined.

There is for example, no reason why, in taking a constructivist understanding of social reality, and developing an evaluation design embracing appreciation of the pluralism of social realities that quantitative tools such as surveys cannot be used. Unravelling the relationship between method and methodology helps in designing evaluations fit for purpose.

The struggle for dominance between various methods is often grounded in a lack of appreciation not so much of the method but the methodologies to which an individual researcher subscribes. A method is in itself not superior or inferior. The real debate has become buried in a discussion of methods. A questionnaire can be every bit as influenced by researcher bias as an interview schedule and its conduct. Qualitative and quantitative methods are associated with these two paradigms, which have different constructions of social reality and therefore of the role of the researcher. This is the place to start.

Positivism

Positivist or scientific approaches to researching social life understand reality as something objective and as a single reality. It exists beyond the influence of individuals and can be understood through social science breaking it into its constituent parts and examining them. Evaluations can look at causative factors and effects in an intervention and so establish the truth about an intervention. The hypothetico-deductive approach means that causal explanations and predictions follow deductive logic. The collected facts prove or disprove a hypothesis.

In this paradigm the researcher can be objective and using the right tools is able to study the effects of an intervention on a population. It is suggested that neither the research process nor the researcher affects those who are investigated. There is no problem of researcher bias as this can be managed through following a clear sampling system for harvesting a study group from the population under investigation.

Post-positivism or constructivism

The alternative paradigm which may be known as constructivist, humanistic, interpretive or post-positivistic describes reality in terms of there being multiple realities perceived and experienced by individuals. The researcher has to try to get close enough to these various groups to accurately record and then report the various realities. There is no sense that there is one reality of greater value or legitimacy over another. The researcher employs methods which get close to those who are being researched in order to best understand their perspectives. This contrasts with the arms length techniques of the positivist researcher. Constructivism is inductive which means that rather than try to test out a hypothesis, proving or disproving it, broader generalisations are generated from the collected data.

Working in a constructivist paradigm there are concerns about the researcher exerting bias. There may be a tendency for a researcher to favour versions of reality and interpretations of events corresponding more closely to their own. In reality working through any paradigm with any methods there should be concerns about researcher bias. Researchers are people and all human actors will bring their concerns and interests to work with them. Patton (1986: 194) writes:

> In evaluation the classic deductive approach is measuring relative attainment of predetermined goals in a randomised experiment that permits precise attribution of goal attainment to identifiable program treatments. In contrast the classic inductive approach is goal-free

evaluation, in which the evaluator gathers qualitative data on actual program impacts through direct observation of program activities and in-depth interviews with participants, all without regard to stated predetermined goals.

This is a quick sketch of differences between positivism and constructivism. The following pages explore some of the ways in which these two paradigms may work.

Experimental and quasi-experimental approaches

This is considered by some the gold standard for evaluative work as it follows a scientific model.

These experimental approaches have causality at their heart, they seek to explore whether there is a cause and effect relationship between a policy or intervention and the target population. It is an approach that is considered to often work well for summative evaluations. It may work best for the evaluation of large-scale policy developments and interventions with big populations. It is costly and time consuming, may not always be precise and generates a number of ethical issues.

Randomised field experimental designs

Here there is a control group, that is a group which matches the members of the treatment group either on the basis of being matched pairs, one member of each pair being allocated to each group, or on the basis that the two groups have broad group features in common.

The control and the treatment groups are treated the same aside from one experiencing the treatment and the other not. The groups may be tested before the intervention which is received only by the treatment group to establish each group's starting points and then again after the treatment to see what changes may have occurred. These are then attributed to the treatment, if they are statistically significant and there is no chance that these changes could have occurred any other way. This is the OXO model outlined in the introduction.

There are a number of variants on the OXO model. For example XO, a single post-intervention test, the supposition being that changes to the treated group will have arisen through the intervention.

In experimental designs, the experimenter has to allocate people into the two groups according to a sampling framework and this raises a number of issues, including:

1. There are ethical issues in human and medical services in allocating people to a non-treatment group: if someone stands to benefit from treatment they should not be deprived of the treatment.
2. If the allocation to groups is not blind and people know they have been allocated to treatment or non-treatment groups they can themselves exert effects. Those in the non-treatment group may try harder in some way to prove the treatment group and experimenter wrong or they may lapse into defeatism because they were not selected for treatment and show worse results than they otherwise might have done. Those who know they are in the treatment group may perform better because they believe in the power of the treatment as opposed to actually experiencing the effects of the treatment itself.
3. The development of treatment and control groups is very costly and time consuming. There are issues with ethical and other review boards in making decisions about control groups.

Quasi-experimental designs

These do not make use of a control group although naturally occurring ones may be found. This approach may make use of a number of designs.

One way is to look at a group which has a treatment, trying to determine its impact by pre and post testing and then attributing causation. However, if people know they are in such a group, what might be the effect of that knowledge?

	Pre-test or pre-intervention	Treatment or intervention	Post-test or post-intervention
Experimental group	O	X	O

Diagram 3: The OXO model with no control

A second approach may be to only post-test the group which has received the treatment. However this is weakened as a design because there is no knowledge of the starting points of that group.

	Pre-test or pre-intervention	Treatment or intervention	Post-test or post-intervention
Experimental group	–	X	O

Diagram 4: Post-test only with no control

The static group comparison is where there is a naturally occurring control group, people with similar characteristics, which does not have the treatment. In this case the treatment group is pre-tested and an assumption made that its starting points are the same as the naturally occurring control group.

Both groups are post-tested and any greater change in the treatment group than may occur through chance is attributed to the intervention. Again there are issues about the knowledge which people have about being in a treatment group or not. As there has not been randomised sampling and group assignment, assumptions cannot and should not be made about the similarity of the two groups and about their starting points.

	Pre-test or pre-intervention	Treatment or intervention	Post-test or post-intervention
Experimental group	O	X	O
Similar group	–		O

Diagram 5: Assumption of similar starting points and testing of end points

Two of the creators of realist evaluation (Pawson and Tilley, 1997: 292) take a stand against the positivist, quasi-experimental and randomised experimental designs. They argue that these are not approaches which can explain causality and change within social programmes, however effective they may be in testing 'washing powders or crop fertilisers'. While these experiments 'allow for the predictions regarding the likely occurrence of future events, they do not explain why particular events happen' (Keat and Urry, 1975).[11] For them adequate causal explanations cannot be achieved by merely observing the relationships between phenomena. The researcher needs to look beyond those initial events that produce change, in order to explain the very process of change itself (Clarke, 1999: 54).[10] As is explored in the section on the realist approach to evaluation there is a need to look at mechanism and context.

Fourth Generation

Some critics of positivist approaches and experimental designs were concerned to explore the social processes which might in part be responsible for the changes which an intervention might bring about. It was the need to discover *why* a change had occurred rather than just finding out that one *had* occurred which preoccupied these evaluation researchers. For some researchers there was a second problem, which lay with the fact that experimental designs and the role of the researcher as experimenter could keep an intervention as a fixed phenomenon when it would have been better for it to have been more responsive to needs.

Early moves away from experimental evaluations and objective outcome measures explored the actual programme activities by using qualitative methods and methodologies. These developments occurred initially in educational research and were concerned with description and interpretation as opposed to measurement and prediction. Early work developed into interpretivist evaluation where social interactions were studied in their social context in an attempt to understand the multiple lived experiences of those engaged in such experiences as opposed to trying to impose scientific modes of enquiry on the social world.

Guba and Lincoln (1989)[12] are seminal in the development of what has become known as Fourth Generation evaluation. This is concerned with putting some parity into the evaluation process by identifying and taking account of the multiple realities of stakeholders affected by an intervention. This tackles one of the concerns with the positivistic approach to evaluation which puts a value on an intervention from the perspective of the evaluator and probably a single stakeholder. Often the creators or managers of the intervention have a vested interest in the evaluation and the intervention. Fourth Generation evaluation addresses several other concerns that emerged from critiques of earlier iterations of positivistic evaluations. These were:

- a dependency on a single view of the issues and the intervention
- decontextualising the intervention, so it was not clear what other variables might be at work affecting the impact of an intervention. This is something which is a key element in the realist evaluation approach, outlined below
- the role of the evaluator as a judge is constructed as 'value free', yet the evaluator working as a natural as opposed to a social scientist was bringing their moral, social, political, religious and economic values to the evaluation. The judgments and recommendations about an intervention were solidly grounded within the evaluator's world-view and may be right, wrong or might overlook key factors. The failure to see the evaluator as human and as constructing the evaluation stripped the evaluation of these effects and the evaluator of this type of accountability
- the positivistic paradigm and the quasi-scientific approach meant that there was an over-reliance on quantitative data which did not allow for a detailed understanding of the lived experiences of those involved in the intervention
- the construction of a pseudo-scientific paradigm which was often locked into the realities of those constructing and managing the intervention (those with power) really meant that the *status quo* prevailed and that dominant policies and ideologies were supported and power remained where it was
- the scientific nature of the positivist evaluation meant that is was somehow untouchable and right. The dominance of the paradigm still prevails in many people's minds. For example, ask any group of students about an evaluation and they will often propose administering a

questionnaire to find out the truth, much as clients commissioning work may do. For some, simple number-based statements of fact seem to be the more truthful and preferred style of reporting rather than putting the figures in some sort of context

Fourth Generation evaluation is called such because it follows after three other iterations of more linear approaches to evaluation which were measurement and judgment based. There are two main phases in Fourth Generation constructivist based evaluation. These are:

Discovery: the description of what is happening, that is the process, programme or whatever it is that is being evaluated. This discovery process takes place with many different types of stakeholder. The circle of the enquiry spreads well beyond the experimental subjects of positivist approaches to a far wider group of people. The stakeholders are no longer subjects, they are co-creators and so through an iterative process of the sharing of views between the stakeholders, with the researcher as a go between, there is the discovery of a more consensual view of the intervention and its impacts. In the language of Fourth Generation evaluation this is the 'hermeneutic dialogue circle'.

Assimilation: the period during which the data accumulated during the discovery phases is analysed to generate a potentially fresh understanding of what is taking place. This is knowledge that builds on from the earlier interpretations of the discovery phase. These two phases can happen in tandem: assimilation informing discovery and leading to new discovery.

Fourth Generation evaluation, working to a protocol meant the views of many types of stakeholders in an intervention were sought.

Within Fourth Generation evaluation the evaluator role is substantially different to that of the positivist counterpart. The evaluator works with multiple stakeholders to create a more consensual understanding of what is being evaluated and a more consensual sense of its value. The interplay of evaluator and stakeholders is seen as a valuable part of a learning process which is an integral part of the evaluation. The evaluation itself is not fully mapped out in advance as it responds to circumstances emerging from the data. Inductive data analysis leads to the generation of theories grounded within or generated from the data itself. The theory of reality is one of 'multiple, divergent and inter-related realities' (Guba and Lincoln, 1981).[13]

The evaluator is not making judgments or recommendations: these too are emergent and the work of the synthesis of stakeholder views.

The evaluation takes account of the local contexts and this means the findings are localised and not generalised. The evaluation when completed, is completed only to that point: there is really no end point and the evaluation process needs to continue.

Constructivist approaches are argued by positivists to yield softer data that are subjective. The constructivist evaluator would in turn argue that the strength of their work came from its pluralism of viewpoints, the depth of the data and the importance of having a synthesised understanding of an intervention. The constructivists would also point to the ways in which positivist researchers could impact their data.

These two paradigms are based on completely different understandings of the world and the knowledge that could be created from social research. It makes it impossible to combine them at the level of paradigms. It is possible to combine the methods of qualitative and quantitative research in order to better meet the needs of an evaluation. Cook and Reichardt (1997: 27)[14] argued for a flexible and adaptive approach; 'there is no need for a dichotomy between method types and there is every reason (at least in logic) to use them together to satisfy the demands of evaluation research in the most efficacious manner possible'. Patton argues for a rejection of methodological orthodoxy in favour of methodological appropriateness to be responsive to the needs of the work.

Realist evaluation

Described by two of it creators, Pawson and Tilley[15] as 'a species of theory-driven evaluation'. This approach, like other evaluative approaches, seeks to understand the nature and effect of a change-oriented intervention. Rather than ask the often rather simplistic question that has driven much recent evaluation of, 'does it work?' realist evaluation asks multiple questions to understand an intervention in a far more nuanced way. It differs from other approaches in that it seeks to understand what elements of an intervention work, with what groups, in what ways, to what degree and in what contexts. It seeks to develop an understanding of an intervention by first hypothesising a range of possible effects on possible groups under various circumstances and then sets out to collect data to test the hypothesis and to theory build.

The intervention which has been developed will have been created and operationalised by multiple hands and so it is not really understood until it can be taken apart. To unpack this, a programme will have been conceptualised, it may have become social policy and in these early stages it will probably have morphed from its original intended form. An intervention will have been put in the hands of managers and practitioners and regardless of the clarity of the communication about the programme it will in the process of being implemented, morph again. There may be a variety of local contextual factors which exert effects, a number of local personalities, interpersonal relationships and participants who will all go on to exert further effects. There may be several of these programmes running in different geographic, social, economic, cultural and political contexts. There will therefore be multiple versions of the same programme.

Realist evaluation acknowledges the potential for these multiple programmes in multiple realities and seeks to discover how and what works, with whom and why. It seeks to understand why there are differentiated programme impacts. It is only by developing these understandings that the programme can be understood (a theory built) and it is understood what best sustains them. This is a way of looking at programmes which acknowledges the importance of the multiple contexts and interpretations. It is a way of looking at programmes which acknowledges that they are themselves live and change the original circumstances or reasons which gave rise to them. In exposing this better understanding of the programme which is in operation this can be used both by policy-makers and practitioners to target resources at what it is they are trying to achieve. Though both need to be mindful that the intervention itself will impact what it is that the programme is trying to change, so this needs to be continually monitored to see if the desired programme effect continues or if there is something else to be done.

Realist evaluation works through several stages:

Stage 1. Hypothesis building

Firstly there is a need to develop a hypothesis about what is happening. Here data about the intervention (interviews, documentary analysis, broader contextual data and sociological theory and research) will be brought together to develop programme understandings. This material is used to assist in answering the following four questions:

1. What are the programme *mechanisms* which might be at work?
2. What are the *contexts* for the programme which might be at work?
3. What are the *programme outcome patterns* which might be at work?
4. What are the *different models of context-mechanism-outcome pattern configurations* which are at work?

Answering this fourth question should give a range of models which can then be tested. This moves to Stage Two.

Stage 2. Data collection
Data is collected by a range of means on mechanism, contexts and outcomes. There is no prescription of methods.

Stage 3.Data analysis
Exploring outcome patterns to see which patterns may be explained by the earlier models (from Stage 1, question 4) developed as part of identifying what context-mechanism-outcome pattern configurations may be at work.

Stage 4. Theory testing
Exploring and revising the initial hypotheses of context-mechanism-outcome pattern configurations.

Realist evaluation makes use of a variety of methodologies and methods; it draws actively on stakeholder inputs at all stages of developing the evaluation plan and its execution. It is pluralist in design and approach. Realist evaluation seeks to explain how something is working and for whom, and so be of value to policy makers and practitioners. The value of presenting these types of findings lies in a high utility and ease of interpretation. It does however take significant commitment to generate the working hypothesis about models of context-mechanism-outcome pattern configurations at work and time to test these against the collected data.

Democratic evaluation

Over the past 40 years there has been the emergence of an interest in democratic evaluation, which is not simply that of using the findings of evaluation as a means to strengthen democracy. For example, the use of findings to strengthen understanding of particular social issues and interventions or get to decisions which are more representative of a wider citizenry. Rather, it is undertaking evaluations in such a way that they represent a plurality of views. The democratic evaluator,[16] ensures that the full range of citizens' views are represented in the design of the evaluation. The democratic evaluator is an information broker working between groups located in different social, economic and political pockets within society. The evaluation is so designed that the methods, techniques and findings are accessible to all non-specialists. The evaluation is itself conducted as a public interest evaluation.[17]

Kushner[18] has refined the democratic model of evaluation. He sees evaluation as a form of personal expression and political action with a responsibility to be critical of those holding political, social and economic power. Kushner's approach questions evaluations working with the frameworks discussed in Chapter 2, logic models, outcomes monitoring and evaluation and theories of change, which are geared to simplifying social chaos and difficulties, and the messy lived realities and perspectives of many people who are subjected to a range of social interventions. He finds the methods and frameworks used for evaluation of many social programmes are constructed in such ways that they come to accept or even justify the social inequalities and difficulties which people experience rather than expose them. These ideas are explored a little further in Chapter 5. For Kushner, as for other democratic evaluators, there is a need to put those often constructed as marginal at the centre of democratic evaluations and develop ways for them to find their voices:

> . . . *each social and educational program can be seen as a reaffirmation of the broad social contract (that is, a re-confirmation of the bases of power, authority, social structure, etc.) each program evaluation is an opportunity to review its assumptions and consequences . . . each program evaluation is an assessment of the effectiveness of democracy in tackling issues in the distribution of wealth and power and social goods.*

Kushner, 2000: 32–3

The evaluator has to make the decision to act more authentically 'to set aside the opportunity is to act more inauthentically, that is, to accept the fictions' (*ibid*).

Working in this way individual evaluations are powerful, but taken together evaluations can become a very powerful societal institution which can bolster or challenge dominant paradigms and distributions of power or wealth. In exploring democratic evaluations the potential is obvious for the ways in which we can use evaluations to better understand social divisions. We can see how evaluations can be used to teach alternative ways of thinking and seeing the world.

Patton argues that if people who participated in evaluations learnt to think evaluatively this would be an asset to them in reconceptualising their social realities which are but short steps to action and strengthening democracy.[19] Chapter 9 develops some of these arguments further, looking at participatory evaluation.

Summing up

This chapter has ranged across several examples of the different reasons for evaluations and differing methodologies: formative and summative grounded within programme evaluation; developmental evaluations; and approaches which seek to generate nuanced understandings such as realist evaluation, or to find ways to help more marginalised stakeholders have voice, such as democratic and personalised evaluation.

Evaluation is a vibrant and developing area of applied social sciences. It is important to recognise that there are a variety of methodologies and what ideologically may drive such methodologies. Such understandings may open options for undertaking evaluations to better meet their purpose.

To close with a provocation from Patton:

> *Not all forms of evaluation are helpful. Indeed many forms of evaluation are the enemy of social innovation. This distinction is especially important at a time when funders are demanding accountability and shouting the virtues of evidence-based or science-based practice. The right purpose and goals of evaluation should be to get social . . . to use tools like developmental evaluation to have ongoing impact and disseminate what they are learning.*[20]

Endnotes

1. Scriven, M. (1991) Beyond Formative and Summative Evaluation. In McLaughlin, M.W and Philips, D. Eds. *Evaluation and Education.* Chicago, University of Chicago Press.
2. Patton, M.Q. (1996) A World Larger Than Formative and Summative. *Evaluation Practice*, 17: 2, 131–44.
3. See also Utilisation-focused evaluation below.
4. Patton, M.Q. (2011) *Developmental Evaluation: Applying Complexity Concepts to Enhance Innovation and Use.* Guilford.
5. Patton, M.Q. 1986, *Utilisation-Focused Evaluation.* California, Sage.
6. Scriven, M.(1991) Beyond Formative and Summative. In McLaughlin, M. Phillips, D. Eds. *Evaluation and Education.* Chicago, University of Chicago Press.
7. Patton, M.Q. (1996) A World Larger than Formative and Summative. *Evaluation Practice*, 17: 2, 131–44.
8. See an account for example Kakkainen, B.C. (2005) Panarchy and Adaptive Change. *Minnesota Journal of Law, Science &. Technology* 7: 59–77. Hilling, C.S., Ed. (1978) *Adaptive Environmental Assessment and Management.* London, John Wiley and Sons.

9. Patton, M.Q. (1982) *Practical Evaluation*. London, Sage.

10. Clarke, A. (1999) *Evaluation Research*. London, Sage.

11. Keat, J. and Urry, R.(1975) *Social Theory as Science*. London, Routledge and Kegan Paul.

12. Guba, E. and Lincoln, Y. (1989) *Fourth Generation Evaluation*. London, Sage.

13. Guba, E. and Lincoln, Y. (1981) *Effective Evaluation*. Jossey Bass.

14. Cook, T.D. and Reichardt, C.S. (1979) *Qualitative and Quantitative Methods in Evaluation Research*. London, Sage.

15. Pawson, R. and Tilley, N. (1997) *Realistic Evaluation*. London, Sage.

16. See McDonald, B. (1987) Evaluation and the Control of Education. In Murphy, R. and Torrance, H. Eds. *Issues and Methods in Evaluation*. London, Paul Chapman.

17. There are two further ways in which commissioners might want to commission an evaluation. One conducted in the public interest is one which is designed in a way to solicit as wide a range of views and interests as possible. The evaluator's mission is that of collecting, aggregating and communicating as wide a range of views as possible. The evaluator is attempting to be independent of any particular viewpoint, would scrutinise any particular standpoint, which they held and declare this. The evaluation is an attempt to represent as wide a range of public interests as possible.

    The second type of use in commissioning an evaluation is partisan evaluation. Here the evaluator acts as the agent of a particular viewpoint, most frequently the commissioner's. The data is collected to illuminate and evidence a particular standpoint, the information and the report presented in such a way to support the commissioner's standpoint. The evaluator in this instance is acting very much as a partisan advisor.

18. Kushner, S. (2000) *Personalising Evaluation*. London, Sage.

19. Patton, M.Q. (1997) *Utilisation-Focused Evaluation*. London, Sage; Patton, M.Q. (1998) Discovering Process Use. *Evaluation*, 2: 2, 225–33.

20. Patton, M.Q. (2006) Evaluation for the Way We Work. *Non-Profit Quarterly*, Spring, 28.

2: Models, Frameworks and Emergence in Evaluation

Introduction

This chapter continues exploring some parameters, understandings and potential ways of working with evaluation. Chapter 1 explored in outline some of the breadth of thinking about different reasons and methodologies for evaluation. This chapter moves down a level from methodological thinking to explore the mechanics used in shaping some types of programmes and evaluations. It explores logic models, theory of change as linked to logic models and as a means to develop a theory of practical community action, and a model of outcomes monitoring and evaluation. These demonstrate how evaluation, monitoring and programme development can be integrated.

These models help to structure thinking about project intentions and impacts, how to define success and think about measures for assessing the extent and degree of success. They are ways of working which may present a challenge to unquestioned assumptions. The models are illustrated with some templates and diagrams that may be useful.

Models are often used at the outset as part of the planning process, but there is no reason why programmes that are mid-term should not make use of these tools. They can help in a process of backtracking and in explaining what is currently being done and why. Working with a theory of change model and, taking some of the explicit questioning from logic models and outcomes, monitoring and evaluation may inject discipline into thinking about a programme which is already underway. They can help explore assumptions and gaps. Selecting a tool of this type can create useful discussion points with an evaluator or support preparations prior to meeting an evaluator.

The chapter closes with the antithesis of a model, that of a discussion of working with developmental evaluation. This reminds the reader of the diversity of evaluation's roles and challenges a model of change as something linear and which is about improvement. In this instance change happens because the social world is dynamic. Issues are complex and for programmes devising innovative ways of working with complex social issues there may be a need to keep moving but to do so guided by robust analysis.

Logic models

These are tools that have been used by programme innovators, managers and evaluators for several decades. They support programme development early on, helping to determine what measures can be used to demonstrate performance and develop an understanding as to how the overall effectiveness of an intervention will be described. Logic models can be understood as a route map helping keep stakeholders close to the project and helping those further away stay in tune with the broader direction of the project and aware of some operational detail. It is a simple way to communicate the essence of a programme.

This section opens with an account of the simple logic model, moves to discussion of different types of logic model, links between logic models and theories, and reviews more complex logic models.

The simple logic model

The model is often expressed as a simple graphic narrative of the inputs, outputs and outcomes of an intervention. It is read left to right, the eye moves from the reason for the intervention, Situation

A (the problem) to the intended impacts at B. Its simplicity means it can be used with a wide range of stakeholders from various backgrounds (Diagram 6).

The elements within this simple logic model are outlined in the boxes below. When building a model the questions in each box need to be explored and fully discussed. The planning process requires full attention be paid to each stage. For programmes already underway trying to articulate the programme in terms of these question boxes will expose gaps and muddle which may have crept in.

Situation: The statement of a problem

What is the problem?

What are the effects of the problem?

What is something of its history?

What happens if this problem continues? What might the consequences be?

Who are those most immediately affected and how are they affected by the problem? Explore severity and any impact on their broader lives.

Who else may be affected by the problem as more distant stakeholders? Generate as comprehensive a list as possible.

Background

What attempts have been made to tackle this problem in the past?

How did these attempts work?

Is there anything positive or negative from these past experiences which might be taken forward with any of the stakeholders in the intended intervention?

Inputs: The resources which the project is using

Develop a comprehensive list of the various resources to be used from the tangible to the intangible. These may be as diverse as knowledge, funding, project staff, volunteers and the location. Explore the inputs from any partners and collaborators.

Part of developing an evaluative understanding of the programme should be knowing how resources can be converted from inputs to outputs and how they affect impacts. Evaluations often involve questioning value for money, programme effectiveness in terms of resources and the social return on investment. This is the type of information funders want and programme managers need.

A resource or inputs review may identify what resources are especially powerful in exerting effect, where there might be more or less need for certain types of resources and which have significant leverage in terms of change.

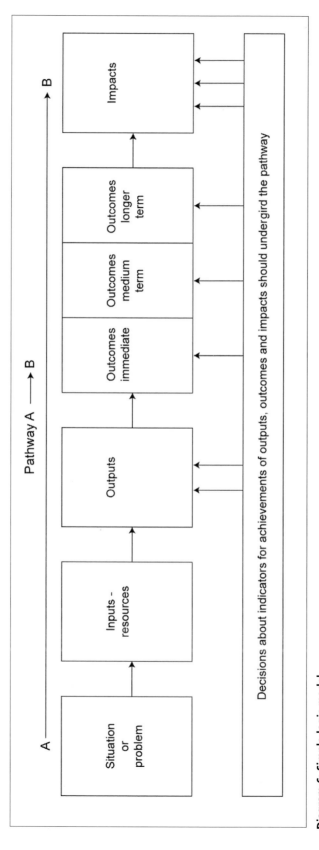

Diagram 6: Simple logic model

Outputs: What is it that the intervention does and for whom?

These could include a range of deliberately created elements such as workshops, outdoor activities, mentoring, team-building games, newsletters, blogs, Facebook pages, action research sets and on-line communication tools.

For projects which are underway there may be other outputs which were not intended but which are outputs. For example, the unintended provision of quiet and reflective space which clients use, conversations with staff or informal peer buddying.

Outcomes: Are the effects those which are intended?

These outcomes need to be definable, so there needs to be evidence that they have happened. They need to be defined in terms of an agreed realistic timeframe. The outcomes need to be within the programme timeframe for them to be measured and to count.

Similarly the outcomes need to be attributable to the project and so need to be traced back into the project's outputs, inputs and decisions about making an impact. If outcomes are linked to too many and different variables then this again makes it hard to evaluate any degree of attribution.

Outcomes for individuals are hard to assess and will need to be evidenced in ways which are tangible, or proxy measures will need to be found, e.g. passing some accreditation. Outcomes could be skills. These need to be measurable or observable. **Awareness**, **insight** and **attitudes** all need to be demonstrable. **Confidence** and **self-esteem** need to be tied to indicators.

Impacts: Bigger and systemic changes

If there are changes for individuals then there are likely to be changes to wider systems because individuals' behaviours and attitudes are likely to affect places, organisations and communities.

Projects should think about the types of bigger impacts they want to make and how these might be achieved, observed and evidenced.

In terms of thinking what it is possible to evaluate as bigger impacts it is important to give this a realistic timeframe and to know that there is a cause and effect pathway from situation, inputs, outputs to the impacts. Some impacts may be after the time frame of the project.

The logic model is an attempt to isolate a cause and effect relationship between certain activities (outputs) and the intended results (outcomes and impacts). It is a systems approach to reaching certain goals. Given that goals will be clearly defined and the logic model will incorporate performance measures from the outset then progress towards goals can be charted from a very early stage in the project's life. Measures developed for the planning process will be used for evaluation.

In diagram 6 outcomes are suggested at various time stages, immediate, medium and longer-term, in addition to the overarching impact. Expressing outcomes in this way is an essential element to knowing if the project is on target and if progress is being made. It is essential when the changes are complex to be able to chart progress towards them.

The simple narrative line illustrated by the logic model is useful in exploring and explaining the intervention with stakeholders. For example, if the work is at the planning stage there can be useful discussions of the route, the types of outputs and their likely links with the outcomes. There can be a review of the outcomes. This will be a reality testing for the planning process and an opportunity to generate more ideas.

The logic model can be treated as a work in progress and new models developed to reflect changes and modifications. Earlier iterations of the model should be kept to help explicate how the project has developed and when any modifications occurred.

There are some pitfalls in working with logic models. These might include:

- it may limit thinking, as the process moves rather linearly from situation A to goals at B. Yet interventions may be very complex and certainly non-linear but this complexity cannot easily be captured. It may encourage thinking in terms of a simplified cause and effect relationship which is not there
- the linearity and seeming smoothness of process may work against more creative contingency planning and may cause discouragement when programmes run less smoothly
- it is possible that project planning may limit itself to existing ideas, for example the types of outputs which are commonly offered in an intervention may be trotted out. It is suggested that beginning with the goals might help shake up thinking by working backwards and thinking more creatively in reverse about the steps needed to get there
- the extent of external influences may not be apparent

There are a number of strengths in this way of working:

- it is a very simple and clear way to explore a whole programme which can be shared with stakeholders
- it is a way to keep the focus on the whole picture: the end points and discussion of some of the programme elements
- it forces thinking about the associations between the various programme elements to ensure a sensible progression between the various inputs and expectations, and that the anticipated outcomes do actually match the needs which were understood as being part of the problem or situation
- from the outset there is awareness of the nature of success through clear statements of outputs and outcomes and the various performance indicators. There is a means to chart success
- logic models are very clear ways to test ideas, many elements having been captured and the associations thought through. If something seems to work then it is easy to move from plan to scale
- logic models can be easily used for replication in other places, having accommodated for any changes in context
- evaluation of programmes can be made far more effective by using the logic model

Life is not so simple as the simple logic model might suggest. It is however useful to be able to distil the essence of a project in this way.

Logic models can have different emphases, and three of these are briefly outlined here: the conceptually based *theory approach logic models* and two applied models, the *outcomes approach logic models* and the *activities approach logic models*. Programmes may make use of all three models at various stages in their development or develop some blend of their own. These distinctions are offered to enable some exploration of thinking which may be useful for evaluators and commissioners of evaluations.

Theory approach logic models

These emphasise the theory of change which informs the development of the programme. The theory of change is explored as a model in its own right in the second part of this chapter. Theory-based models require time spent in exploring the reasons and understandings which gave rise to the development of the programme and the ways in which various elements have been selected to take the programme from situation identification to the outcomes and impacts intended to provide some resolution to the problematic situation.

These models may be found more at the outset of programme planning as they are ways of testing speculations as to how the project may work. The theory-based logic models draw on a variety of sources of data to inform their theories for action. These could include sociological theory, other empirical research, earlier pilot or demonstration projects or work from other programmes:

> *A program is a theory and an evaluation its test. In order to organise the evaluation to provide a responsible test, the evaluator needs to understand the theoretical premise on which the programme is based.*

Weiss, 1998[1]

The diagram below offers a template for a theory based logic model. The emphasis is on working to surface all assumptions driving the programme.

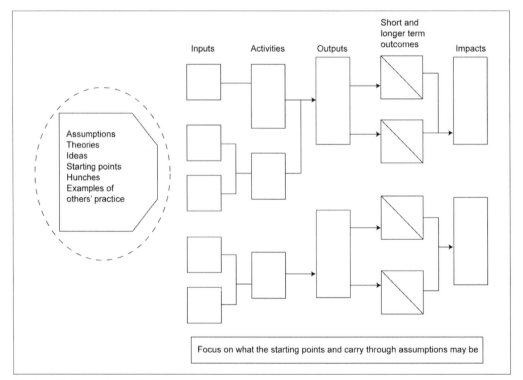

Diagram 7: Theory-based logic model

Outcomes approach logic models

These models emphasise the links between specific programme activities and outputs and outcomes. It is a way to very explicitly trace the project's causal linkages. These should be robust enough to make sense at the drawing board stage when any fallacious or erroneous assumptions may be noticed.

Causal links can be checked through meeting the performance indicators and the evaluation once the project is underway. What may have been assumed at the outset as a strong causal link may be found wanting. It is important for the evaluation to explore why this is so.

A diagram below outlines a type of template which can be used. Each activity should have a clear output and lead to a specific outcome. There may need to be occasions when two or three outputs are linked to an outcome, this needs to be diagrammed. This again is an area which the evaluation can explore. For example, were these assumptions correct? Is one output more important than another?

Activities approach logic models

Like the foregoing models these models link activities to outcomes in a causal way but the emphasis here is in really describing in rich detail the types of activities and how they are undertaken. This works at a very deep level of operational planning. This may be used for work planning with staff, and so may have value at early stages of development.

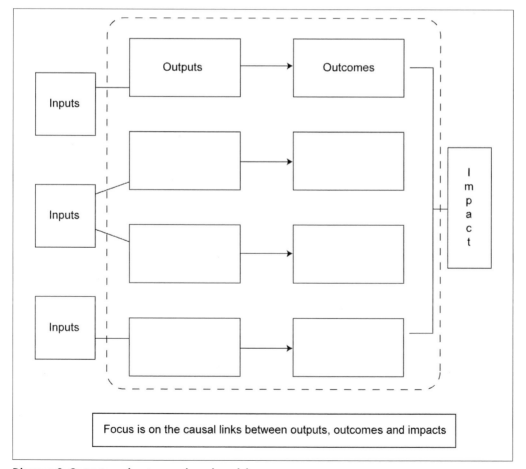

Diagram 8: Outputs and outcomes based model

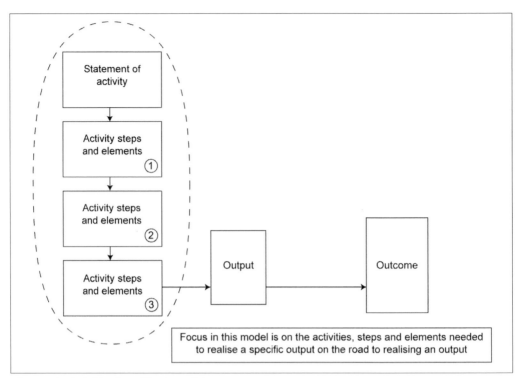

Diagram 9: Activities based logic model

It is also useful to use with others who wish to replicate the programme. For programmes wanting to demonstrate that very particular programme effects are related to a particular model of activity then this high degree of specification and the ability to check on the assumed causal links between activities and outcomes will be important.

The evaluation process and logic models

The use of logic models shapes the focus of the evaluation questions. The overarching evaluation questions, see Chapter 7, should be clearly stated using the statement of the situation and the intended impacts of the programme.

The structure of the logic model provides scaffolding to the evaluation creating an ease of focus on programme elements. For example:

- there is clarity about the inputs to the programme and a means to trace inputs to outcomes
- it is possible to focus on use of resources, effectiveness of resource use and assess the types of inputs which have greater value in delivery of programme outputs and outcomes
- there is clarity about links between activities, outputs and their causal links with outcomes, which creates something definite to be tested
- there are statements about the intended outcomes and a timeframe offered for different types of outcome and impacts. This drives the evaluative questions as to the degree to which programme expectations were realised and within what timeframe
- the statement of the problem and the statement of outcomes allows clear evaluative focus on the ways in which, and the extent to which, the programme may have been right in its assessment of the problems and solutions
- the unexpected will stand out and should be explored evaluatively

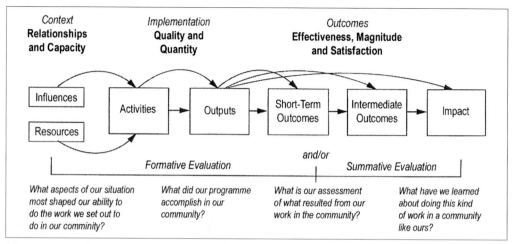

Diagram 10: Evaluation and the logic model [2]

The diagram above illustrates the ways in which evaluation at formative and summative stages weaves into the programme. The evaluation will be able to draw on any data which has been collected as performance indicators. This is an issue explored in more depth below.

Theory of change

Some logic models are combined with theories of change. Weiss, a key exponent of the theory of change[3] defines it quite simply as having a theory of how and why an initiative works. The evaluation of the intervention supports or refutes the theory of change and explores why it was or was not the case that this theory or model worked. This statement is unpacked in the next couple of paragraphs.

Programme designers need to develop a theory about the change they are trying to achieve, that is moving from a problematic situation to outcomes and impacts which remediates that which was problematic. With community based or social initiatives there are often many complex factors at work. A theory of change is about unpicking these elements in order to be able to project a logical pathway for the change, whether forward from problem to outcomes or working backwards from the desired outcomes. Programme developers need to define the steps they want to create along this pathway. In so doing they will be surfacing their assumptions about the building blocks needed to realise the intended changes.

Any failure in stating these steps along the pathway for change means it is less likely that a programme will see the realisation of its end goals and it will be harder to evaluate the efficacy of a programme. The statement of problem, goals and the elements constituting the projected pathway sketch out the programme's theory of change.

While this sets the scene, a more complete theory of change:

> . . . *articulates the assumptions about the process through which change will occur, and specifies the ways in which all of the required early and intermediate outcomes related to achieving the desired long-term change will be brought about and documented as they occur.*[4]

These early and intermediate outcomes, along with the final outcomes need to have specific indicators attached to them. This way it becomes clear if the outcomes have been realised in full or part. Having this insight helps keep the work on track.

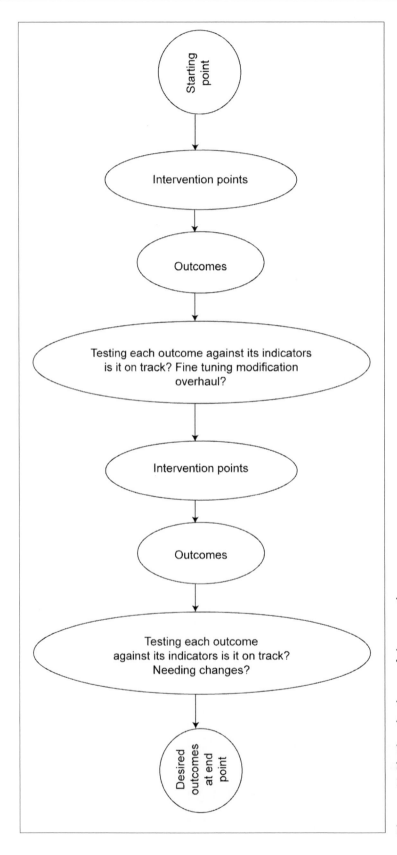

Diagram 11: Plotting the theory of change path

In working with a theory of change model the indicators are really important. Every outcome at every stage needs to have clearly defined indicators. At every step of the way each outcome will be tested against its indicator to see how and what progress or degree of realisation has been reached.

Every indicator needs to be defined in great detail. This makes it more useful for evaluation and to assess the extent to which the programme is on the right track.

Writing about defining indicators Anderson suggests three questions to ask of each carefully defined indicator. These are:

1. Who or what is the target population of change?
2. How much change has to occur on this indicator for us to claim to have successfully reached the outcome?
3. How long will it take to bring about the necessary change in this indicator in the target population?[5]

Developing a theory of change has advantages:

1. Injecting clarity into programme planners' thinking, and so capacity to articulate what they are doing, thereby better enabling evaluation of what is happening.
2. Paying attention to realising goals and what the early and intermediate steps towards their realisation may be injects focus on what needs to happen or to be done.
3. Working backwards from the goal may stimulate more creative thinking.
4. It keeps all stakeholders and evaluators focusing on what is being attempted and understanding the steps to get there.

In articulating a theory of change project planners will be stating their assumptions. These assumptions should be tested by the evaluators as the theory of change is an essential component of the intervention. It is the glue which binds the whole intervention. The planners may draw on research or other literature, their past practices or the work of others. This needs exploring with the evaluation team for its value, accuracy, underlying logic of the assumptions and to check that all stakeholders are making the same assumptions about the change process.

The questions evaluators direct at each theory of change and its assumptions will vary by project.

Building theories of change will:

- expose any inconsistencies in the logic of the project
- make explicit the understandings of social change which can be tested through the evaluation
- generate knowledge, because something clearly stated is being tested
- set criteria for success which evaluators can use to chart progress and explore short-falls
- explain how resources are to be used
- set common goals and targets on the way
- help scope and manage expectations about what is achievable and what may be outwith the scope of the intervention

Developing a theory of change makes much about the change work explicit. This will highlight where outcomes may emerge which were not intended and this may be explored as to why this was so. It allows for exploration of where something may work well or less well with certain groups. It is a better articulated way of working.

Outcomes monitoring and evaluation

As a form of evaluation this is one often used by funders and voluntary organisations within the UK. It gathered momentum during the 1990s and 2000s. It is driven by understandings of the importance of monitoring and evaluation which include:

- defining an acceptable version of success for an intervention for stakeholders
- being able to answer the questions about whether something worked and how well it worked
- proving the value of an intervention
- being accountable for funding
- demonstrating value and value for money
- gathering data for learning and future improvements
- developing interest in the quality of what is being done
- underscoring the importance of planning within voluntary sector interventions

As a form of monitoring and evaluation this is often presented as atheorectical, there is little concern about why something is being done, what is driving it or what it may prove. It is a style of evaluation which is very grounded within an organisation, is heavily concerned with building an evaluation and monitoring strategy but it is at risk of not seeing the larger picture.

This has been a pervasive way of thinking about evaluation within the Third Sector so it is offered here as another example of an approach.

1. The starting point is to know what it is that the organisation is trying to achieve. This may be known as a mission statement or an overarching aim. This broad statement needs to be developed at the outset, or failing that, to be drawn out from an existing project. The statement of purpose is the impact which the project seeks to have.
2. It is not possible to operate at the level of a statement of purpose or impact. So more specific aims need to be developed. In terms of the evaluation these are the outcomes the project wishes to realise. The outcomes are statements of what success would look like should each of the aims be realised.
3. The specific aims are broken into smaller objectives, two or more for each specific aim. These objectives are things to be done and which build to the realisation of the specific aims. Each objective equates outputs, things the organisation does, with the resources which it has or has raised.

This can be expressed in Diagram 12. The left hand side shows the elements commonly found within a business plan or statement and on the right, the elements of a monitoring and evaluation plan.

The performance indicators included in each box should be understood as staging posts on the way to realising a project output, outcome or impact. The indicators are ways in which the partial success of something can be described. As indicators are met in full or part it is understood by those undertaking the monitoring and evaluation that progress is being made. If there are problems in completing an indicator this serves as a diagnostic tool. It may help in identifying organisational or project blockages so a fresh approach or more effort may be directed at that indicator. It may be a signal for re-thinking some element of the intended work. It may be an alert that something is not working or indeed, may not be possible.

Performance indicators can be turned into grid form and set against a time-line and used to check off progress and developing success. The performance indicators can be used in the monitoring and reporting processes of an organisation.

At the day-to-day level output performance indicators can be used to show, for example, attendance, throughput of beneficiaries, the number of services and the types which are provided and so on. The outcome indicators are larger success measures and the performance indicators would be checked on a more periodic basis. These would for example suggest that a cohort of beneficiaries had developed skills or become more confident as evidenced by some piece of accreditation being acquired.

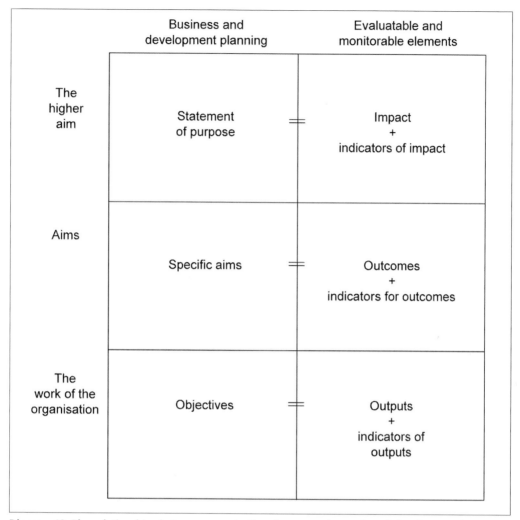

	Business and development planning	Evaluatable and monitorable elements
The higher aim	Statement of purpose ⇌	Impact + indicators of impact
Aims	Specific aims ⇌	Outcomes + indicators for outcomes
The work of the organisation	Objectives ⇌	Outputs + indicators of outputs

Diagram 12: The relationships between organisational purpose, its work and the elements for monitoring and evaluation

Just as the products of an organisation are monitored, so in this model its inputs need to be monitored and where possible tied to particular outputs so effectiveness in resources terms can be captured. Performance monitoring can be undertaken by staff and perhaps other stakeholders such as service users. An evaluation would be likely to draw on some of this data generated through the monitoring process. The evaluation would be able to use the monitoring data as evidence of success and performance. The evaluation will be exploring the programme against its self-set statements of aims (outcomes) and purpose (impact). Evaluation design is explored in Chapter 7.

Monitoring and evaluation conducted against this framework is something focused internally on the organisation's performance. This may yield rich data on particular types of programme performance and generate data on value for money, but it is unlikely to create more general material or to lead to the development of an articulated theory of change. This framework has other internal uses, it can for example be used to check over time for any mission creep, and that what it was setting out to do, the organisation continues to do. This is especially important when there is soft or project-by-project funding and organisations may adapt their activities to match funders' interests.

Finally this type of framework is useful in being explicit, to check what continues to be possible and current, especially at time of scarcer resources, and it can help with priority setting.

Evaluation should be used to feed back into a review of aims, objectives and outputs and inform the business development cycle as well as be used to inform funders.

Developmental evaluation

There is of course no framework for developmental evaluation. It is the antithesis of the above structured models. It is a way of working with a variety of methods, formal methods such as interviews and questionnaires and a range of facilitative approaches to encourage the surfacing of assumptions and thinking. The programmes needing developmental evaluation eschew clear, specific and measureable goals upfront because clarity, specificity and measurability are limiting, such a programme does not seek standardised inputs, uniformity of outputs and clarity of causal links as the previous frameworks have emphasised.

The following table from Westley, Zimmerman and Patton (2006)[6] illustrates the differences in approach between developmental and traditional evaluations.

This highlights the importance of the evaluator working in the 'here and now' with the team which is developing and innovating the programme under review. This will require the evaluator to have certain characteristics and skills, to have high level communication skills, capability to ask difficult questions to draw out assumptions and challenge under surface models which drive the innovation,

Traditional	Developmental
Render definitive judgments of success or failure.	Provide feedback, generate learning, support changes in direction.
Measure success against predetermined goals.	Develop new measures and monitoring mechanisms as goals emerge and evolve.
Position the evaluator outside to assure independence and objectivity.	Position evaluation as internal, team function integrated into action and ongoing interpretive processes.
Design the evaluation based on linear cause-and-effect logic models.	Design the evaluation to capture system dynamics, interdependencies, models and emergent interconnections.
Aim to produce generalisable findings across time and space.	Aim to produce context-specific understandings that inform ongoing innovation.
Accountability focused on and directed to external authorities, stakeholders and funders.	Accountability centred on the innovators' deep sense of fundamental values and commitment.
Accountability to control and locate responsibility.	Learning to respond to lack of control and stay in touch with what's unfolding and thereby respond strategically.
Evaluator determines the design based on the evaluator's perspective about what is important. The evaluator controls the evaluation.	Evaluator collaborates with those engaged in the change effort to design an evaluation process that matches philosophically with an organisation's principles and objectives.
Evaluation results in opinion of success or failure, which creates anxiety in those evaluated.	Evaluation supports ongoing learning

Diagram 13: The features of traditional and developmental evaluations

skills as a facilitator, skills in synthesising complex information, capability to work within a dynamic context and to work with ambiguity. All this is needed on top of possessing a good range of traditional and more participatory research methods and pattern recognition.[7]

The evaluator will have to be able to hold the boundaries for the innovation team so that they recognise the evaluation in action data for what it is, an additional source of critical thinking to add to the decision making process. The evaluator will need not to be fearful of working much more closely within an organisation than is usual. They will need the skills to share knowledge, ways of working and thinking with the team engaged in the innovation and development work.

This is not a role to be played by any professional who wishes to stand on the sidelines nor one who wishes to retain any mystique about the work of an evaluator as a very particular expert.

Summing up

This chapter has explored in some detail several ways organisations might make use of frameworks, or not a framework in the case of developmental evaluation, to better state and explore what it is going to do and what it is doing. The more mechanistic of the frameworks can be geared to a more managerial approach of proving the worth of a project. Some of the other tools may be used to explore and develop theories or understandings of an intervention and work more creatively towards outcomes and understanding the processes leading to outcomes.

Endnotes

1. Weiss, C. (1998) *Evaluation: Methods for Studying Programs and Policies.* New Jersey, Prentice Hall.
2. See Kellogg Foundation (2004) *Logic Model Development.* Michigan, W.K. Kellogg Foundation. p.36.
3. Weiss, C. (1995) Nothing as Practical as Good Theory: Exploring Theory-based Evaluation for Comprehensive Community Initiatives for Children and Families. In Connell, J. et al. Eds. *New Approaches to Evaluating Community Initiatives: Concepts, Methods, and Contexts.* Washington, DC: Aspen Institute.
4. Anderson. A. (undated) *Theory of Change.* New York, Aspen Institute.
5. Anderson. A. (undated) *Theory of Change.* New York, Aspen Institute. p. 5.
6. Westley, F. et al. (2006) *Getting to Maybe: How the World is Changed.* Canada, Random House.
7. See Gamble, J. (2008) *A Developmental Evaluation Primer.* Canada, JW McConnell Foundation.

3: Evaluation, Learning, Change and Organisations

Introduction

Patton[1] writes there is little value in an evaluation if it is not used and this is an essential message of this book. Evaluations can present enormous opportunities to a variety of stakeholders as individuals and as members of organisations and programmes, at all stages of the work from inception of an idea, through execution and completion. At best there are opportunities for capacity building and development of individuals and organisations and effective programme learning. This chapter explores some of the learning potential which evaluations can generate.

Patton suggests engagement in the process of evaluation is in many ways more useful in the longer-term than the findings of an evaluation which may have a more limited shelf life. Receptivity to the process encourages learning and potential for change. Evaluation is a way of thinking and can help the on-going development of an organisation and its work.

> *Effective evaluations also prepare organisations to use evaluation as an ongoing function of management and leadership.*

Kellogg, 2004: 2[2]

Organisational and individual learning outcomes from evaluations are not always listed as benefits or even intended outcomes; the learning potential from evaluations can get glossed over. This chapter teases out such learning and describes how an evaluation feeds back into an organisation's growth, as part of its feedback loop. The chapter introduces and explores some ideas about:

- learning
- learning and change through participation
- organisations
- readiness
- organisational learning
- the value of evaluation
- working with change
- learning as a tool for working with change
- developing communities of practice

Learning

There are many definitions of learning, types of learning and models of learning and this is not the place to explore learning theories. Learning is a natural state or there would be no individual or community survival, it is something done daily and not something which has to be masterminded into a formal programme and delivered. It is 'a process by which behaviour changes as a result of experience'.[3] The following paragraphs touch on a couple of elements about learning which are useful to consider when thinking about working with evaluations and their outcomes.

There are several models of individual learning which have features in common. Firstly people learn when there is a need or a want to know something, this is the motivation or the drive to learn or discover. Secondly, people learn when they are actively engaged in something, making discoveries through trial and error. Thirdly, people learn when they gain feedback from others which may help

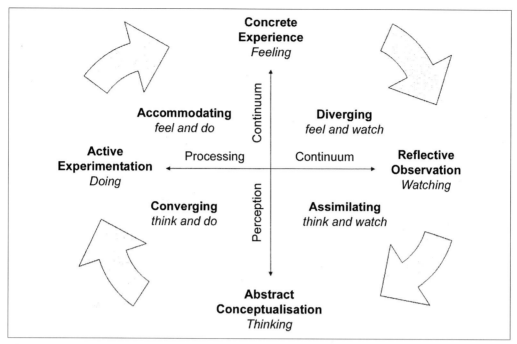

Diagram 14: Kolb Cycle of Learning

them shape actions and understandings. Finally, people try to make sense of information and reactions to their own errors and observations.

A dominant explanation of the learning cycle was developed by Kolb and published as a four-stage model in 1984. The elements listed above appear in this model. People work through each of these stages on the cycle as they learn. According to the Kolb model, people have a dominant learning style related to stages on the Kolb learning cycle. They will be predisposed to learn in this way. As people mature as learners they will develop skills and aptitudes enabling them to work with all the stages around the learning cycle.

A variant on Kolb's cycle is Rice's learning domains.[4] Rice argues that rather than work a step-by-step cycle people work a series of cognitive and kinesthetic operations in tandem; people are not tidy thinkers. People will try to gain feedback as they are engaged in an action; they will sense make as they are engaged in an action, seek feedback and work towards corrective action all at the same time. The model is one of ripples of behaviours and thoughts which interact with each other.

There are a number of advantages in knowing one's own learning style, for example, does one learn best by assembling information and formulating ideas, by testing out personal theories, by trying something out and seeing, with the eye of an experimenter, what works? Knowing personal strengths and possible developmental areas is important in developing as a more balanced and therefore effective learner.

Just as knowing one's own learning style is important, so is knowing those of one's colleagues.[5] It is important not to be dismissive of others' ways of working, for the importance of the strength of a team and so as not to miss opportunities when issues or developmental situations need to be approached. Failing to appreciate colleagues' exploratory style of developing knowledge and dismissing it as jumping in where fools fear to tread will impact a team's potential for success. Awareness of various ways of learning is important and especially when evaluations are in process

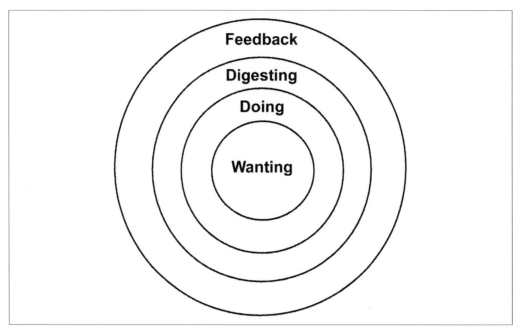

Diagram 15: Elements of learning [4]

and there are opportunities to look at the familiar in different ways. Skilled evaluators can bring to the surface things that have been buried, and opportunities to work with an outsider's insights on a programme or an organisation at issue should not be overlooked.

Learning is not a single person activity (Lave and Wenger, 1991)[6] it is something which happens in a social context. People need feedback on what they are doing in order to make sense and to modify or develop what they are doing. This has implications for thinking about evaluation and the learning which is possible from evaluation. The importance of social context can be thought about in relation to participatory approaches to evaluation. The nature of evaluation itself is a form of feedback, working with the outputs of evaluation, for example deliberately working with findings in the context of a group learning situation and thinking about ways in which organisations can become places of learning. It is important to ensure that there is a climate within an evaluated programme or organisation which enables this learning. These elements are explored below.

Learning and change through participation

> *The best evaluations value multiple perspectives and involve a representation of people who care about the project.*

> Kellogg, 2004: 2

Chapter 9 deals exclusively with participatory evaluation, a form of evaluation with its own methodology, values, repertoire of conventional and more innovative methods. Participation in evaluations may stop short of being fully participatory. Participation is located here in this chapter on learning to underscore the importance of learning within a social context and the gains from participatory approaches. Other issues, democracy, voice and political choices are the meat of other chapters.

Depending on how they are set up, evaluation processes offer rich learning opportunities. For example, participation at the earliest stages of determining the research areas and questions can enable a broader understanding of a variety of perspectives and lived experiences of the various stakeholders. There will be opportunities for people from a variety of backgrounds to gain insights into others' interests, what they value and are concerned about in the development of the intervention. Engaged and insightful working will follow from sharing these types of learning opportunities.

If an evaluation is run in a participatory fashion, there can be significant gains in terms of cross-group learning about substantive issues, sharing perspectives and knowing how to communicate with and work with other groups. There can be capacity building, as individuals from different groups learn new skills, acquire new strengths and some develop leadership skills within their communities.

The evaluation will benefit from having been developed according to multiple stakeholder perspectives. It will give rise to more meaningful outputs and outcomes and different stakeholders are likely to feel commitment to the findings and recommendations and the ensuing changes.

Organisations

Much can be written about organisations but a few points are offered here about organisational identities and resistances.

Organisations are human creations, their cultures, values and ways of operating are shaped by the people within them. This means that they can morph, more deliberately change or get stuck in a rut, just like individuals, 'because patterns of human interaction produce further patterns of interaction' (Stacey, 2005).[7] Organisations are vulnerable to the ways in which people behave. They are open to learning and changing, if the people who make up those organisations opt to work with new concepts, to change their behaviours and the ways in which they interact.[8]

As organisations are human-made, so humans come to invest them with much of their own identities and anxieties. Work is a fundamental element for many people in shaping and defining their identities. It has a role way beyond that of paying the bills.

> *A group's identity is linked to defining its primary task – its reason for existence (Rice, 1963) . . . in organisations caring for people, identity and tasks are often linked to ideals and ideology . . . since the personal meaning of the work tends to be vested in the ideals underlying the choice of working methods, it can be very anxiety-provoking to question them. Instead of space to reflect on what is most appropriate for whom, there is often polarisation around right or wrong . . .*

> Roberts, 1994: 114[9]

A lengthy quote but one making several essential points; people and organisations become closely inter-linked, defining and being defined by each other. The nature of much working life is a relentless march, there is no time to stop, reflect and to support individual professional and organisational learning.[10] The fear of the interloper, or evaluator, lies in its potential to reveal something which is not working well, that it may pass judgment and threaten the organisational and personal sense of well-being and identity.

For some organisations and the individuals within them this can be especially alarming if they have actively increased the stakes. Quoting again from Roberts:

> *Many teams and organisations are set up as alternatives to other, more traditional ones, by someone disaffected by personal or professional experience or other settings. However, identity based on being an alternative, superior by some ethical or humanitarian criterion,*

> *tends to stifle internal debate. Doubts and disagreement are projected, fuelling intergroup-conflict . . .*

An evaluation can be triply risky in these situations. It may threaten to expose inner discord, expose the mythologising of being different, demonstrate that there is little difference with respect to other organisations and their work, that there is little basis for feeling superior or that there is little impact from the work being performed. Evaluation is a high-risk event. Any adverse comments can, so long as organisational defences stay intact, be dismissed as a failure of the evaluation to understand.

A set of allied points are made by Senge (2006).[11] He writes that people are 'trained to be loyal to our jobs – so much so that we confuse them with our identities'. For Senge, people's loss of perspective means that their vision becomes narrowed. They align only with the job or role and cannot see over the parapet into the wider system. They are unable to take the purpose of the job, the organisation and the system into account. Hunkered down within personal silos they seek to blame others, within the same organisation or outside the organisation, when something goes awry.

This is faulty thinking, which will perpetuate the problems, create resistances to learning and to contemplating doing things differently let alone doing things differently. There will be no recognition of the need to do anything differently, and there will be casting about to blame someone else because there is no sense of the whole organisation.

This narrow fixation of the individual can be extrapolated to the whole organisation. Organisations become stuck looking at single events and episodes and be unable to look at the bigger system and the emergence of patterns. Unable to see beyond the moment, the organisation will be like the frog,[12] which boils in its own juices as the environment around it changes and heats up. However, organisations do not have to be stuck, they can begin to learn as is explored below.

Readiness

A key question is how ready an organisation may be for an evaluation, to participate in evaluatory processes and to work with the learning opportunities which are offered. If there is not readiness then no matter how effective the evaluation team, internal or external, or how effective a form of self-evaluation, it will not work.[13] The process will be construed as invasive and unhelpful, the outputs will be seen as, at best, missing the point or at worst as an affront.

> *Without seeking to know about its effectiveness, a group inevitably loses its capacity to adapt and to develop ... the importance of fostering a spirit of enquiry within organisations, so that evaluation can become a tool for learning from experience.*
>
> Obholzer and Roberts, 1994: 168[14]

The next section explores organisational learning and how organisations may be made more receptive to learning.

Organisational learning

The nature of learning organisations has been much debated. It was a concept developed and popularised by Senge in the early 1990s when learning was linked to managing in an ever-changing environment. Such needs for pro-activity and adaptation have not changed. Senge's vision for a learning organisation was:

> *. . . organisations where people continually expand their capacity to create the results they truly desire, where new and expansive patterns of thinking are nurtured, where collective aspiration is set free, and where people are continually learning to see the whole together.*
>
> Senge, 1990

Senge's vision has been criticised for being vague, how is it possible for an organisation to action such sentiments? Various commentators have noted that there is no actual definition of a learning organisation.[15] Dale argues that rather than trying to find a blueprint for the learning organisation it is an understanding of its features that is important. These elements will appear in different organisational contexts in different ways.[16] Organisations do not just become learning organisations, they need to work at developing into them. According to Senge, as organisations get larger they can get more fixed and it can be harder to undertake this development. A way around this is to break an organisation into units, some of which may take on the form of learning organisations, sharing back services with other units. Other organisations may downsize to stay more innovative and to become and remain as learning organisations.[17]

In a learning organisation the culture is one where the learning of individuals and the organisation is valued and supported. This means 'a no blame culture' where there is not a process of trying to seek out an enemy, whether within the organisation or outside, but having a sense of being part of a larger system. A learning organisation has a grasp of the bigger picture, a sense of itself as a sub-system within a system and of the passage of time and patterns within the organisation and beyond. A learning organisation does not move from event to event, episode to episode in a process of correcting problems and issues. This is to engage only in single loop learning and corrective actions. It tries to have a larger and longer term strategy. A learning organisation questions its assumptions and finds answers and ways to develop in the patterns which it detects within and around it. This is to engage in double loop learning. A diagram of these two learning loops is offered below.

A learning organisation does not bind itself into highly regulated procedures and practices, it allows for fluidity and learning from feedback on its actions. It has open communications within the organisation and beyond. It is innovative and responsive and puts resources to work to be so.

Cultures, organisational or otherwise, are human-made and it is important that those creating the culture of an organisation are committed to enabling individual and organisational learning. Features of such a culture would include:

- investment of time and other resources in individual development
- rewarding individuals as solution seekers

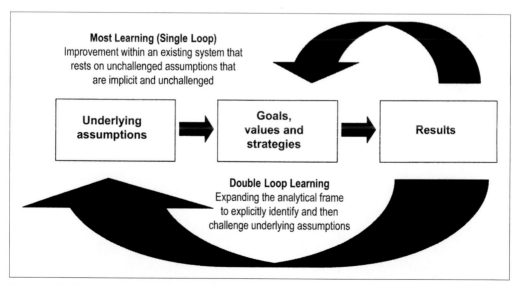

Diagram 16: Single and double loop learning

- trusting that individual learning will contribute to the development of the whole
- finding ways to pull individuals' learning into whole organisational learning
- trusting:
  - in individuals' capacities to problem identify and solve and to encourage such behaviours throughout the organisation
  - in change and development as emergent and having the patience to enable this by putting aside the need to manage through top-down controls
  - in processes of experimentation
- not managing anxieties through denial and control but surfacing and working with them
- valuing the concept of personal mastery. People need to invest in becoming good at what they do. This may be through a range of learning activities, not all formal training, but trialing, reflection and discussions with others. Personal mastery contributes to the good of the organisation
- creating and nurturing the spirit of enquiry within the organisation and with other organisations
- adopting systems thinking and seeing the bigger picture over the longer-term
- supporting double and triple loop learning, doing more than correcting any shortfalls, finding out what prompted shortfalls in the first place and exploring assumptions and theories in use[18]
- promoting the idea of communities of enquiry within the organisation and enabling the sharing of its work

There are of course barriers to developing learning organisations, for example, a lack of buy-in to individual learning and the concept of organisational learning, a lack of shared vision and limited open communication. There is a need to find a means to link individual and collective learning, to link learning with other organisational structures and the direction of the organisation. This is a lot to articulate. There may be barriers of time and other resources to investment and a lack of collective will to make such investments lead to changes. There are pitfalls in enabling individual learning in an unaligned organisation: it will backfire with individuals pulling in different directions. The ask is great in an organisation developing towards having an organisational learning culture.

Organisational learning has to be grounded within the organisation as a normal element of everyday life. The flip side of the heavy investment in learning is that an organisation which does not learn may get stuck, may at worst fold or at best drift into undertaking tasks or using its energies in ways that do not advance its mission. For learning organisations questioning, change and transformation are normal ways of being.

The value of evaluation

'To benefit from experience it is essential to make something of it' (Leiper, 1994).[19] Evaluation adds value to organisations in pushing learning on several fronts. It is a means to help organisations make something of their experiences, it holds a mirror up to the organisation reflecting back an image of what it is doing. It is feedback from people coming into the organisation but without being steeped in the organisational context. They undertake an independent enquiry. In these ways the organisation gains feedback on what it is doing through the process as the evaluators with their different backgrounds ask questions and reveal different visions of the organisation.

Engagement in the evaluation process will provide opportunities for learning a range of new ways of thinking and new skills. This evaluative thinking and evaluation processes can be incorporated into future ways of working and decision-making. The findings may themselves present many opportunities for change.

Working with change

Change is understood within the context of organisational learning and evaluation as an essential element to survival, evolution of services, improvements to services or use of resources. Change is assumed as a positive outcome of learning and from evaluation. However, Dale notes that some organisations and their people will seek stability as opposed to change; she calls this 'dynamic conservatism'.[20] Whether this is actually possible except in extraordinary circumstances and probably with some independent stream of financing is hard to imagine. This 'dynamic conservatism' Dale argues is not to be confused with stagnation. Stagnation is paralysis and systemic inability to change which will lead to demise. Change and assumptions about change need to be tested within organisations as it is a source of significant anxiety.

Individuals and their organisations can be resistant to change, experiencing panic and anxiety because it is known that change will open up taken-for-granted ways of operating which have become routinised and unquestioned. It is a way to not think about what is done on a day-to-day basis.

Senge finds resistance to learning and therefore to change leads organisations to push 'harder and harder on familiar solutions, while fundamental problems persist or worsen'. It is what he calls 'what we need here is a bigger hammer syndrome'. Organisations failing to engage in learning, developing systemic understandings and change are at the mercy of repeated applications of the same solution. He finds that:

> The most insidious consequence of applying non-systemic solutions is increased need for more and more of the solution. That is why ill-conceived government interventions are not just ineffective they are 'addictive' in the sense of fostering increased dependency and lessened abilities of local people to solve their own problems. This phenomenon of short-term improvements leading to long-term dependency is so common, it has its own name among systems thinkers – it's called 'shifting the burden to the intervention'. . . all help a host system only to leave the system fundamentally weaker than before and more in need of further help.
>
> Senge, 2006: 61

This last observation while important in helping understand organisational resistance to change is also important in thinking about the impacts organisations may themselves be having on those they seek to help. For example, organisational refusal to engage in learning, to open up to a participatory approach to evaluation or to accept the findings of an evaluation can be damaging to those it seeks to serve.

Change is complex and can stimulate difficult feelings but it needs to be conceptualised as something:

- organic and normal, not be presented as something which is pathologised and labelled as threatening to individuals or an organisation
- which can be worked with in an organisation in a participatory way, with all levels of the organisation involved and not as something which is driven top-down or imposed on people without their consideration
- which is allowed to be emergent, evaluated as it proceeds, can be corrected and also questioned. As in the process of double and triple loop learning
- which has a sense of direction and a focus and is not a reactive flailing about
- which does not blame or undermine what was done in the past, but builds on the past or at least acknowledges the past. It is important in working with people's sense of identity and connection with their work

- which is understood to be a challenge and threatening for some people and for whom time and space is allowed to explore these feelings
- which is backed by resources and time to enable the development of new working practices

In working with change, a likely outcome of the evaluation process in a receptive organisation, it needs to be labelled as a positive and the right conditions created for working with it.

Learning as a tool for working with change

A way of working with change is to do so constructively in learning or research-based activities. This may be done within an organisation or across several organisations. For example, the outputs from a cluster style evaluation[21] might enable several organisations with similar issues to work together on a learning project to meet their collective needs. There can be gains from using different organisational or programme contexts as lenses through which to gain insight and perspective on similar problems.

There are several ways to work with learning for and about change:

- creating an in-house association of learners
- action learning
- developing communities of practice

In this context change is conceptualised as an iterative and dynamic process. These modes of learning about and with change are explored below.

In house associations of learners

Cross-organisational groups explore and consider how to take forward findings from an evaluation. Grounding the exploration of problems and the development of a change strategy within the organisation will make the work more participatory and accepted.

Working associatively will increase individuals' and organisational capacity and buy-in. People will have a sense of being represented and feel invested in the working group. It will generate more innovative solutions than one person working alone. It will gather insights across the organisation and create a more rounded view of the issue and possible solutions. It will prevent tram-line thinking which can arise from one person working on an issue or when people from the same functional group work on an issue.

Action learning

Reg Ravens[22] is attributed with developing 'action learning'. He first used the term in 1970s but did not define it so as not to confine this form of learning. Action Learning emerged when Ravens observed his scientific colleagues engage in a form of enquiry with each other to explore the problems each faced in their research. Given the nature of research, no one other than the particular scientist with the problem had the same depth of understanding. Ravens observed the scientists asking each other intelligent and provocative questions, assuming that the problem holder, the one with the issue, had the answers or solutions. Ravens considered that learning was derived from a combination of what was already known and the exploratory and detailed questioning of what the scientist was doing. In this way a new understanding and knowledge was being developed which helped move the scientist and so the research work along.

Ravens took this way of working into his career as a manager and as a management academic, concerned that 'business schools were teaching an inexhaustible avalanche of lofty hocus pocus'. He wanted to re-balance book-based and research-based knowledge with action-derived knowledge. Action Learning is a call to action but also a demand for sober questioning and reflection. It requires

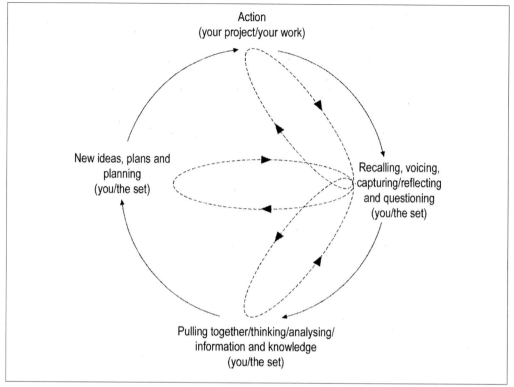

Diagram 17: The action learning cycle

an on-going revisiting of the problem in light of actions taken and a more sophisticated cycle of learning. This is the double and triple loop learning process outlined above.

Participants in an Action Learning set divest themselves of their usual assumptions, their tendencies to half-listen, desire to offer advice or seek quick solutions. Each participant takes a turn to tell the others of a real and complex problem or issue. The problem teller, or in Ravens' phraseology, problem holder, is assumed to know how to address the issue. This tacit knowledge[23] just needs drawing out. Those listening do so actively until the problem holder has finished. They ask questions which genuinely ask the problem holder to explore their issue from other perspectives. The questions are not advice in disguise. The open questioning moves the problem holder to think about the issue afresh, and to surface their ideas and assumptions. The problem holder determines an action which they think will be useful and tries to undertake this after the meeting. The results of the actions taken are brought back to another meeting of the Action Learning set. The actions are reflected upon and more questions asked. This again puts the problem holder in the situation of questioning their assumptions and any limitations in their thinking.

The process of taking action and reflection on the ensuing outcomes continues for a few rounds. The group helps an individual move and encourages more bold action than might be taken alone.

Action Learning as a way of working with findings from an evaluation or experiences generated through an evaluation process is a powerful way for individuals within an organisation to take control, work with findings, issues surfaced through the process and suggestions, and find their own developmental solutions. It is a way to stimulate the work of learning and change without imposing on people.

Developing communities of practice

This is based on the understanding that people learn in a social context and not just alone. Communities of practice are a deliberate coming together of a group of people 'who engage in a process of collective learning in a shared domain of human endeavour'... people 'who share a concern or passion for something they do and learn how to do it better as they interact regularly' (Wenger, 2007).[24] Working with the normal human desire to be together is a way of working and learning together which can generate interesting sharing and developmental practice.

The members of a community of practice share information, knowledge, insights into practice and their skills. They learn from one another. They develop tools, resources and ideas together and for use together. They can test these in their own working environments and bring their learning and insights back to the group for further exploration. These communities can help people to undertake deeper reflection. Like Action Learning sets it legitimises as well as stimulates enquiry into personal practice and innovation. Again, this is an interesting and supporting way to work with findings which emerged from an evaluation or evaluative process.

Summing up

This chapter is a pause in the process of thinking about what an evaluation may be and what forms it takes. It has directed the reader's attention to some wider issues, the importance of the institutional context in which the evaluation is taking place, the type of learning culture the organisation or programme may have and the value of double and triple loop learning.

For any evaluation to have use it has to be able to work with receptive individuals and organisations. The evaluation needs to be framed as an element of organisational learning which stakeholders understand to be useful and normal. The evaluation needs to be appreciated as a way to help give shape to experiences to date and as support in making sense of experience.

Wanting an evaluation and wanting it to be helpful will be very much influenced by how it is framed by individuals and organisations. Finding it helpful and useful will be very much about the capacity for engagement with the process, taking learning from the process and finding ways to leverage the findings.

Endnotes

1. Patton, M. (2001) *Qualitative Research and Evaluation Methods*, London, Sage.
2. Kellogg, W.K. (2004) *Logic Model Development Guide*, Michigan, Kellogg Foundation.
3. Merriam, S. and Caffarella, R. (1998) *Learning in Adulthood.* 2nd edn, New Jersey, Jossey-Bass.
4. Rice, P. http://www.londonmet.ac.uk/deliberations
5. Likewise there is value in understanding one's own and colleagues' communication styles and team-working styles. It is important for example to interpret a directive or dominant communication style as just that, a dominant communication style backed by no more knowing than that of other team members with less dominant communication. Failure to interpret and appreciate correctly will weaken opportunities for problem solving and development for the whole team. See http://www.e2rc.net.
6. Lave, J. and Wenger, E. (1991) *Situational Learning: Legitimate Peripheral Participation.* Cambridge University Press.
7. Stacey, R. (2005) *Experiencing Emergence in Organisations.* London, Routledge.
8. Squirrell, G. (2011) *Engagement in Action* Ch. 4. Lyme Regis, Russell House Publishing.
9. Roberts, V. (1994) The Self-assigned Impossible Task. In Obholzer, A. and Roberts, V. Eds. *The Unconscious at Work.* London, Routledge.

10. Argyris, C. and Schon, D. (1978) *Organisational Learning: A Theory of Action Perspective.* Reading, MA: Addison-Wesley. and Schon, D. (1983) *The Reflective Practitioner: How Professionals Think in Action.* London, Temple Smith.

11. Senge, P.M. (1990) *The Fifth Discipline: The Art and Practice of the Learning Organisation.* London, Random House.

12. The parable of the frog. A frog hops into boiling water and notices, it jumps out. A frog which sits in a pan of water on a stove but is unaware of its external surroundings will find itself boiled alive as the water is heated up. So an organisation which fails to notice what happens around it will not survive. Cited in Senge, P. *The Fifth Discipline.* London, Random House.

13. Robson, C. (2000) *Small Scale Evaluation.* London, Sage.

14. Obholzer, A. and Zagier Roberts, V. Eds. (1994) *The Unconscious at Work.* London, Routledge.

15. Kerka, S. (1995) *The Learning Organisation.* ERIC; Garvin, D. (2000) *Learning in Action.* Boston, Harvard Business School Press.

16. Dale, M. (1994) Learning Organisations. In Mabey, C. and Iles, P. Eds. *Managing Learning.* London, Routledge.

17. Senge, P. (2006) *The Fifth Discipline.* London, Random House.

18. Theories in use are those things individuals and organisations actually do as opposed to their espoused theories, the things that they say they do. There may be procedures set up on the basis of espoused theories, but actually other procedures are performed, there will be a mismatch. Evaluations will reveal mismatches such as this.

19. Leiper, R. (1994) Organisations Learning from Experience. In Obholzer, A. and Zagier Roberts, V. Eds. *The Unconscious at Work.* London, Routledge.

20. Dale, M. (1994) Learning Organisations. In Mabey, C. and Iles, P. Eds. *Managing Learning.* London, Routledge.

21. Several evaluations of different but related projects being undertaken exploring similar issues in order to make comparisons.

22. Ravens, R. (1998) *The ABC of Action Learning.* London, Lemos and Crane; McGill, I. and Beaty, (2001) *Action Learning.* 2nd edn. London, Routledge; Pedler, (1996) *Action Learning for Managers.* London, Lemos and Crane.

23. Knowledge which is gained from experience, listening to, working and watching others in the work place. It is not necessarily something formalised. It is often an under-valued and under-rated knowledge.

24. Wenger, E. (2007) *Communities of Practice: A Brief Introduction*, Communities of practice. http://ewnger.com/theory/

4: The Ethics of Evaluation

Introduction

Ethics have their own chapter and are separated from the politics of evaluation. Evaluations have a particular role to play in social research. They are intended to inform decision-makers; they may stimulate change or facilitate decisions to terminate programmes and practices. Evaluations are part of strategic reviews of policy and provision, affecting the development of both. They can materially affect people's lives as beneficiaries, as workers and volunteers. These are weighty contributions abounding in ethical issues.

There may be a tendency in the cut and thrust of an actual evaluation to dismiss some of the following discussion as aspirational. However, given the possible consequences of an evaluation which backfires, doing damage at worst and at best proving a wasted opportunity, any such inclination should be resisted.

The chapter works through a number of ethical issues in the design and operation of an evaluation, from issues of access to those of confidentiality. It explores issues in working with vulnerable groups and young people. It explores issues in field relations and in leaving the field.

It is important to be familiar with ethical guidelines for conducting evaluations. Examples can be found at the websites of UK Evaluation Society, http://www.evaluation.org.uk and the US Evaluation Association, http://www.eval.org. Additional guidelines are available to social researchers in disciplines of health, criminology and the social sciences. See for example, the British Society of Criminology, http://www.britsoccrim.org/codeofethics.htm. Any evaluations conducted by an independent contractor such as research company, institute or university should also have their own guidelines to follow.

The chapter explores four areas:

1. Ethics and design
2. Ethics and entry into the field
3. Ethical decisions and different stakeholder groups
4. Ethics and exit

Ethics and design

There are a number of elements from an ethical perspective to take into account when designing the evaluation.

Purpose

The first has to be developing with the commissioners the reasons for undertaking the evaluation. Way before proceeding with any discussion of contracts it is important to know why the evaluation is sought. This should apply to all types of evaluation, internal, external and self-evaluation. It is important for the evaluators to decide if they want to go ahead if there is a micro-political or structural review element to the work which might cost jobs and loss of services. Evaluations should be geared towards improvements, developments and knowledge generation, not undertaken as a covert way to get service cuts and redundancies on the agenda.

Risk

There are a number of elements of risk to explore in an evaluation and a formal risk assessment should be developed as part of the evaluation design (see Chapter 7). The risk assessment should include ways in which the evaluation may adversely impact stakeholders. This might include everything from not being able to complete an evaluation because there were insufficient data, through surfacing potential damaging information about a service provider, to distressing issues arising for participants in an evaluation. There may be particular types of risk associated with different designs and methods and with different substantive areas. It is important to explore the implications of design decisions.

Review boards and ethics committees

There are likely to be formal arrangements to review any evaluation plan as part of a process of approving it as research. It is important to be clear that participants in the evaluation will not be damaged in any way or exposed to risks of damage through their participation. An assessment of risk or for example upset or distress is necessary as is the consideration of ways to help manage such risks. Anything involving health, access to medical information or any treatment related evaluations will be especially subject to strict controls which will need to be met.

Contracting

This is a key element in the process and it is covered in a separate chapter. If the contractual basis for the evaluation is not right then there is little chance that the evaluation will be successful and the likelihood of learning from the evaluation will be slight. It is essential in the process of contracting that the evaluator understands completely what is being commissioned and why. Evaluations are not replacements for performance management and an evaluator has every right to turn down a contract for work that is more about performance management than evaluation.

Evaluation design

There are several elements to consider in designing an evaluation. Firstly the choice of methodology and then how the methods should fit the evaluation questions and be appropriate to respondents. This may mean working on several types of tools and seeking ways to make them accessible to different stakeholder groups.

Secondly it is important that there is sufficient time to create a robust design, trial questions and accommodate setbacks. There should be sufficient time designed into the evaluation to do the work properly, to work effectively and respectfully with participants, explaining carefully what is involved, taking time to answer their questions and ensure every participant feels heard and not exploited for the information they can offer. Time needs to be allocated for checking facts and perhaps testing interpretations. Misrepresentation because of the pressure of looming milestones is not a reasonable excuse.

Ethics and entry into the field

There are a number of considerations at the outset of an evaluation. Several of which are explored below.

Negotiating access

A crucial consideration is that of how best to negotiate access. It is important that there is not an assumption that stakeholders should answer questions just because they are stakeholders. Evaluations are not assaults on people's time and attention just because they are involved in a programme as participants or as its staff. Assuming participants gain some benefits from a programme does not entitle an evaluator or commissioner to presume they have a right to garner experiences from those participants.

The process of negotiating access is multi-layered and on-going. The evaluator needs to earn the on-going right to access. Key gatekeepers may permit access for the evaluation because they have no choice, it might be a funder requirement or contractual term or it may be about their sense of identity as a community's gatekeeper. However, entry rights should not be assumed to flow from a gatekeeper and everyone at every level needs to be asked. Permission to collect data is an on-going negotiation, both within one data collection episode and over multiple episodes.

Accurate representation of the evaluation

Closely aligned to gaining access is the way in which the evaluation is represented and expectations are managed as to what the evaluation might achieve. It is quite wrong to present the evaluation as setting out to achieve something outside its remit. The evaluation is primarily a research activity. It may be a special kind of applied research activity to generate knowledge to inform decisions, but the evaluator is not the decision maker. Suggesting the evaluation *may* lead to a programme or organisational changes is one thing, to try to specify the changes or state that it will lead to improvements, more funding or programme expansion is another. While these may be attractive reasons for someone to be involved in the evaluation as a respondent, it is misrepresentation.

Coercion

There should be no suggestion to any potential respondent that there will be any negative repercussions from declining to be involved in the evaluation. Respondents should not feel compelled to provide certain information nor to answer questions in particular ways.

Informed consent

This is an interesting area and one to which there is a high chance that simple lip service may be paid. Robson writes: 'I have the suspicion that sometimes the form is used more for the protection of the evaluators and their organisations (not a negligible consideration of course) than to safeguard the interests of clients or participants'.[1]

The principle is that everyone who is asked to provide information should agree to do so having understood what the data is being collected for, the purpose of the evaluation, its research questions and how the data will be used.

Discussion of informed consent often involves the issues of confidentiality and anonymity, who will access the data and how it will be stored and disposed of.

This is a lot of ground to cover but it is important that this is done. People are giving their time and access to their opinions and they need to know why they are doing this. People deserve a thought through and full explanation. It is important that explanations are presented so they are intelligible to all types of stakeholders, there must be no fudging the issue by using jargon, or trying to intimidate through technical language or pulling rank.

Potential participants need to know how long they will be involved in something (for example an interview, focus group or test) and what is required of them. They need to know about any costs they might incur (which they should not) any possible negative or other consequences of their involvement and any risks and benefits. They need to know about any incentives or provisions for their comfort, for example, travel costs reimbursed, any small payments or gifts in kind and any provision of refreshments.

It is important practice to present this information both in written form and orally and to allow time for questions.

Potential respondents are asked to sign consent forms, to confirm that they understand what is involved and that they agree to be involved. There are several issues here. Does everyone who receives the written material read or read English? Do they understand what was written in the way it was intended? There may be a need to have information in alternative languages and certainly a need to back anything written with an oral explanation and the chance given for them to ask questions. Then a form may be signed. Even so the evaluator may be concerned that there is not full cognition or that the respondent is agreeing because they feel they have to. Examples of consent forms and of project explanations can be found at http://www.e2rc.net.

Informed consent is not a one-off action. There must be ongoing checking to ensure that participants want to continue, for example, checking willingness again before a second interview. Along with explaining about the evaluation, to gain informed consent people need to know that they can opt out in full at any point, and that they can choose to not answer a question or do some activity. They do not need to justify to you why they make these elections. Part of informed consent should be telling potential respondents whom to contact if they have concerns or complaints.

There are times when it is even more complex to gain informed consent. These include working with young people and vulnerable groups.

Informed consent and young people

Children and young people are a very special category. Parental or carer permission for children's participation may be sought depending on the age of the child or young person, the type of activity to be undertaken and any detailed information which is needed about the individual child. Children and young people should be asked for their agreement to be involved if they are of an age to understand and to assent. There may be particular rules to be followed in working with young people, and particular child protection policies in some organisations, and these must be consulted. No young person should ever feel coerced into being involved in any research or evaluation.

Informed consent and vulnerable groups

There are concerns about working with more vulnerable adults who they may not understand or may feel pressurised to give their assent. Examples may be older people, people accessing services or in residential or care facilities, or people held 'captive' in some way by their need eg health, handicap or age, or by the direction of the state. What is involved needs very careful explanation and the right to not be involved needs to be reiterated.

Respectfulness and incentivisation

In the preceding section on informed consent, it was noted without comment.

> *They need to know about any costs they might incur (which they should not) any possible negative or other consequences of their involvement, any risks and benefits. They need to know about any incentives or provisions for their comfort, for example, travel costs.*

So now let us unpick this. Participants should not lose by their involvement in any evaluation research. For example, if an organisation wants to commission an evaluation and wants its staff to be involved, then they should be released from their work duties in work time. They should not then have to make up the missed time and if possible their work should be covered for this period. They should not have to return to their desks to sort out issues or stay later than their usual working day. This applies to paid staff and to volunteers. This has resource implications and needs to be budgeted for in the costs for the evaluation. The onus is on the commissioners to factor these costs into their budget.

Budgets should include expenses such as travelling to an interview or focus group. If the research cannot be taken to the participants then they should be reimbursed for any out of pocket payments. This may also involve paying for the costs of a carer for a relative who has to be watched or paying for or providing crèche facilities. It is important not make assumptions about participants' financial willingness or capacity to contribute to an evaluation.

Participants should be worked with in a respectful way and this includes making sure that physical needs are met, by providing an appropriate location for interviews or group sessions, ensuring refreshments and the like. I once had a researcher who was asked to conduct a day of interviews in a windowless and very small storage cupboard. This was hardly a demonstration of respect for the participants' time, the evaluation or the researcher.

The provision of incentives is an interesting issue. Does the provision of something constitute payment for information and generate a sense of obligation on the part of the respondent to try to give the evaluator what they think they might want? The construction of the research tool and the skills of the researcher should tease out any internal inconsistencies in the responses of the participants, but the respondents should not feel under pressure to respond in a particular way because some small incentive is offered.

The nature of the incentives is also an issue. For example a small payment to a population of homeless people and substance users at a day centre as part of an evaluation about their experiences of relapse prevention support may generate concerns that the money might be used to buy drink or drugs. Are the evaluation team and the contracting body, which will be footing the overall budget, then condoning substance use amongst this group? Should the incentives be created in a way to control the future behaviours of those who might be respondents? Does the research team and commissioning body have a right to do this? Incentives raise many ethical issues.

Ethical decisions and different stakeholder groups

It is important in the design process to undertake proper research to identify all stakeholders who may be touched by the issue or programme under scrutiny. These may be stakeholders who are more peripheral, they may be stakeholders who are considered harder to reach or be more marginalised because they are young people, older people or are in some way less visible in society. It is important to know who the stakeholders are and to have very clear reasons for their exclusion if they are to be excluded.

It is important, if programmes and interventions are running within multicultural communities to ensure the evaluation is designed to match the needs of diverse groups, undertaken in ways that are culturally sensitive so that different groups can participate and so they feel comfortable to do so. For example, perhaps taking account of the need to run single sex focus groups to attract some respondents and enable them to talk, or making sure that research tools use the right language, or have people interviewing, co-leading or running group activities from the communities from which participants are drawn.

Safety

Evaluations, as other types of research, must be undertaken in ways that provide the participants with a sense of psychological and emotional safety, after all a psychological contract is being entered into with them; for their time and assistance, you are ensuring that they are not harmed.

There are likely to be concerns in a number of cases, for example, evaluations which are run with small numbers of respondents, those which are run as internal evaluations or self-evaluations, those where respondents may be dependent in some way on the programme or organisation which is under review or may be considered as vulnerable. All evaluations need to ensure that there is confidentiality and anonymity for the data, that procedures are explained, people's needs taken care of and that those running the evaluation have a clear plan and that they are trained.

A recent example I was offered of a poor evaluation was that of a study of a programme to support young gay men with suicidal ideation and self-harm issues. The research organisation appointed an interviewer who was a young gay man and it was therefore thought would have affinity with the respondents. However he had little research training and demonstrated no basic empathy about the issues that might prompt the young men to self-harm.[2] He was reported as moving through the research questions like an automaton and of course opened up a number of difficult issues for the young respondents who had been previously supported through their bouts of significant personal crisis.

The organisation concerned complained that following the evaluation interviews they needed to provide supportive counselling to a number of the young men who were 'left out to dry' after the interview with a number of complex and complicated feelings about their recent and past self-harm or suicidal experiences. The respondents were not debriefed or offered anything at the close of the interview by the researcher of the research organisation by way of closing down that which the interviewer had opened up.

Physical safety and safety from accusations are also concerns in managing evaluations, the safety of researcher and participants being important issues. Research staff do need to be trained and their backgrounds checked before they work with vulnerable groups.

Working within the field an evaluator may confront some of the following issues.

Overt and covert data collection

There is really no reason why an evaluation should include any covertly collected data. There may be exceptional situations such as observations of the effectiveness of some deterrent to criminal activity, but a focus group with people defining themselves as ex-offenders may work just as well and would include some accounts and analysis as to why something could act as a deterrent to themselves and others.

As a rule of thumb there should be no covert data collection. Significant arguments would need to be mounted as to why a situation might require this. This will be an issue in gettting a proposal through an institutional review board.

What to do when there are issues of harm, self-harm or criminal activity

Some social policy and programme evaluations will be taking place with groups of people who are vulnerable and who may have been engaged in activities which have led to self-harm, harm to another or crime. It behoves any researcher to explain that they are obligated to report to an appropriate authority any concerns they may have. This needs to be said up front when seeking informed consent. This may be a reason why someone would withdraw their involvement.

Ideally if a respondent has opened up these types of issues with the evaluator they will be willing for the matter to go to someone with capacity to deal with them. The evaluator and respondent may go together. Irrespective of the evaluator's particular training when playing the role of an evaluator they are not there to undertake therapeutic work with a respondent. This would be intra-role conflict for the evaluator and confusing for the respondent and probably neither role would be properly executed.

Children and young people

It is important the data collection tools and types of inquiries match the abilities and interests of young people and children. They should not be put under pressure to sit through lengthy data collection tasks nor be asked to do something too difficult. Activities should be designed which are age appropriate, have breaks, inherent interest and some scope for enjoyment and learning.

If children and young people do not want to be involved no pressure should be exerted. It is easier for young people and less intimidating if the research is taken to them. Scheduling should take into account their needs, not the evaluators'.

Vulnerable adults

Likewise vulnerable adults should not experience the data collection as disturbing or pressured. Activities should be appropriate to their skills and capacity. Data collection should take account of the need for breaks.

Photo and video disclaimers

Informed consent is one thing, taking photos and video material of people is another. If there is a need for visual data capture, possibly for programme promotion, to illustrate a report or as a display of the types of creative activities involved in the evaluation then it is really important that people's written permission is sought. There need to be full explanations as to what the material may be used for. Participants may be keen to help or interested in being filmed, but despite their motivation they need to be aware that images have a life of their own, beyond the time of the immediate, and that they may well be seen by people who recognise them. It may be that later on they do not want to be known as having been involved with a particular type of programme. They should think ahead. It is costly to try to change websites and brochures if someone later changes their mind.

The captive

There are a number of ways in which people are captive. They may literally be incarcerated in institutions, prisons, secure centres or mental health facilities. They may be hospitalised and highly dependent.

In these contexts it is likely that interviews will be a prefered evaluation method as they will possibly yield more than a survey for various reasons including possible concerns respondents may have about staff reading what has been written, difficulties in returning the survey and potential respondents having the right conditions and capacity to complete surveys.

There are a number of issues in asking people about their experiences in such places. It is important to emphasise confidentiality of the data and anonymity in the write up. It is important to make clear what the interview is about and that if there are any times when someone does not want to answer they can stop. It is possible that some question will spark concerns, recollections or upsets.

There may be issues about people feeling compelled to oblige the staff by speaking with the evaluator. It will be important to tease this out and to ascertain if the interview is being used as an opportunity to advance another agenda. Data needs to be triangulated in all cases and especially so in these situations.

Evaluators may be used to carry a particular message, or the evaluation used as an opportunity for getting a sense of justice. It is important that the evaluation tools have their own internal checks and that the evaluator is experienced and alive to such possibilities.

The researcher will need to be clear about their own boundaries and that of the interview. The role being played is researcher not therapist, friend or being there to help. There will be institutional rules to adhere to.

Group interviews are possible but there may be dynamics within the group. Because people are living in close proximity and may have low feelings of trust towards others makes it more difficult to generate honest and open answers about some areas of life and experience, in group interviews. It is important that group interviews do not put people at a disadvantage or increase any sense of personal vulnerability.

Opt outs

Respondents should know that they are able to opt out of any element of the evaluation, for any reason. It may be that the evaluation makes them feel uncomfortable or that they simply do not have the time.

Respondents are under no obligation to offer any reason as to why they want to leave. If they are willing to offer an explanation it may be helpful as data, although not admissible in the report writing, or as feedback on the conduct of the evaluation unless explicitly requested as such.

Respondents should also know that they can have any interview scripts, notes, tapes or questionnaires which relate to them withdrawn from the data pool. The only proviso is that if a survey was completed anonymously it would not be possible to withdraw their data without then needing to dump all the other questionnaire returns. This would not be reasonable or practicable.

The evaluation team

It is important that there is professional and supervisory support during an evaluation, especially during the field work period because it is likely that this will be one of the most fraught times for the evaluation's director and field staff and for the lone evaluator. This is where there may be a number of issues: the risk of clashing demands for time, various opinions being offered which may not square, potential conflicts between evaluation team and contractor, difficult emergent issues in the data and ethical concerns to negotiate. Where people are working with vulnerable groups, or where field staff are inexperienced then opportunities to re-align boundaries and to express distress or stress are important.

Anyone undertaking evaluations should have regular debriefings on the progress of the work, any emerging concerns and issues, and any experiences in the field which are proving taxing. It is healthy to re-establish perspective. It is important to factor this type of professional support into the evaluation design and budget.

Ethics and exit

Use of the data

It should be needless to say, but the data should only be used for the purpose for which it was intended. The ownership of the data should be negotiated and contractually agreed. The most usual arrangement is that the data belongs to the research team, given that any other arrangement would make a mockery of assurances of confidentiality and anonymity. If this is an internally driven evaluation, steps should be taken to try to replicate this arrangement. This is important given potential concerns that colleagues in this type of evaluation may have in giving material to fellow workers.

It should be clear throughout the process who will see the data. There is no reason why this should be anyone outside the evaluation team, and the names of who sees the data should be made available to respondents. For example, this could be included in the invitation to potential respondents.

There should be a clear statement about how the data will be used. This should be explained before people become respondents. For example if a report is to be written will there be any way that an individual respondent, institution or geographical area could be identified? If not then how will this be done?

It is important to check with respondents and those commissioning the evaluation if they want everything presented anonymously. There may be concerns that effective practice will be lost in anonymity and that some people will not be credited for the good work that they do. Ways around this could be found and could include named case studies or vignettes in an otherwise anonymised report.

Storage and destruction

Data should be held in a secure place, under lock and key and within a secure office. Data should be managed according to the Data Protection Act 1998, http://www.legislation.gov.uk/ukpga/1998/29/contents.

There should be an agreed date when the material will be destroyed. Data does need to be accessible for verification of any concerns or issues up to that point.

Personal information held about people or information in which projects can be identified should be disposed of as confidential waste. The Freedom of Information Act 2000, http://www.legislation.gov.uk/ukpga/2000/36/contents should also be consulted.

Leaving the field

After each data collection activity individuals and groups should be thanked. If possible contact should be maintained with all stakeholders to tell them what is going on, as is appropriate to their needs. It is important that stakeholders feel that their contribution has been valued and that they have not just been used by the evaluators; for many stakeholders this may well have been an experience of those in official or authority roles.

It is important that any issues or concerns are cleared up before the evaluation team leaves the field. There is an obligation to fellow professionals to make sure that subsequent opportunities for evaluation and research have not been queered by poor practices.

Writing up issues of confidentiality, anonymity and veracity

Unless otherwise agreed the reporting should not name individuals, programmes or geographic areas. The evaluators need to remove any elements which might lead to identification even if this means not using what otherwise would have been arresting quotes or other data.

The evaluators have an obligation to check facts, to triangulate the data so that there can be grounded interpretations. They have an obligation to ensure conclusions emerge from the data not just their preconceptions. They have an obligation to ensure that recommendations are aligned with the purpose of the programme being evaluated and are possible.

Sharing the findings

Good practice suggests that those involved in the evaluation should be party to the findings of the evaluation. There can be some layering of the findings, for example, if some matters pertain to internal and operational issues these may not need to be shared outside the organisation.

In sharing findings it is worth thinking about the benefits that might accrue to other organisations in the field, local authorities or umbrella organisations. Yes, the evaluation may have been paid for by one organisation or through its fund-raising efforts but the consideration of the wider benefits from sharing the evaluation should be considered.

Correcting facts and mis-interpretations

There should be opportunities for stakeholders to correct errors of fact. A procedure of interim, final draft and final reports or variants on this allows for these types of corrections. If these changes materially affect the analysis then this will have to be re-worked and as appropriate fresh interpretations developed. The corrected facts and interpretations should be included in any final reports and disseminations.

The issue of mis-interpretations are important. The evaluation team has an obligation to listen to the concerns of those who feel mis-represented. However the evaluation team may feel that given they have had opportunities to collect multiple data sets and to triangulate the data that their interpretations are correct and so should stand. There may need to be some record in the report as to why there may be a difference of opinion.

Summing up

This chapter has explored a number of ethical considerations in the development and running of an evaluation. Some of these considerations are dictated by law, for example, the Data Protection Act 1998, others by professional codes of ethics or by review boards, for example that of the Department of Health. Some considerations are fashioned from values of equity, respect and an appreciation of power relationships and power imbalances.

Endnotes

1. Robson, C. (2000) *Small Scale Evaluation*. London, Sage.
2. There are many reasons why the researcher may not have managed to strike the right note with the respondents. One could speculate that the issues were too personally uncomfortable for him and he was emotionally defending himself as he did the evaluation interviews. He may simply have been too inexperienced and felt out of his depth, may have been inexperienced and not realised his role performance was poor and so on. A key lesson from this is to check what is being done early in the fieldwork so interviewers and other field staff do least damage, can be helped and the data can be the best it is possible to gather.

5: The Politics of Evaluation

Introduction

This chapter starts from the position that 'Evaluation research should be understood as inherently political'[1] (Taylor and Balloch, 2005: 1). It explores several ways in which evaluations should be understood as socially and politically constructed, politically driven and their outputs politically expressed.

Evaluation operates within a socially and politically constructed world, examining constructs and judging them. Evaluation, like the services it examines, is human-made and not a given: it is politically and socially constructed. Evaluations often report on proposals, services and representations which are themselves constructed within contexts shaped by inequalities and which may endorse them. Just as evaluation is political, how it is fashioned, enacted and used has political meaning. There are many politically driven and loaded choices made in framing, undertaking and working with an evaluation.

The chapter considers what is political in the world of evaluations in three ways:

1. in the ways evaluations are constructed and implemented in relation to social policy development and governance
2. the micro-politics of being grounded within an organisation or programme and in the ways the evaluation and evaluator are constructed
3. at the personal level of the impacts which the evaluator's own self and world-view creates constructs and exercises effects

Evaluation research may be intended to be neutral but it is not, it is human. There is much at stake in terms of decision-making that flows from an evaluation and this exerts a pressure on the evaluator and on those commissioning an evaluation. An evaluation is often attributed as having a lot of weight in decision-making; whether this is true or not in actuality is debatable and down to individual circumstances. But this perception of being powerful exerts an effect. This perceived power can be used in various ways. For example, the choice of methodology is an exercise in managing this power: a fully participatory evaluation is a political decision. This particular methodology means power is shared amongst stakeholders for formulating and undertaking the evaluation. The findings may not be supportive of some groups' interests and subsequent actions may change the ways in which resources are shared between groups. Only those committed to such democratic approaches of shared power and decision-making would embark upon this. Chapter 9 explores this form of methodology.

This chapter explores less fully participatory approaches to evaluations, investigating relationships between evaluators, stakeholders as research respondents and as commissioners of evaluations. It encourages the reader to reflect on the various decisions and choice points where power and politics may shape an evaluation.

Putting evaluation in a broader socio-political context

Within the public domain evaluation is inextricably linked to the politics of policy development, decisions about the use of public resources, government and governance. It would be naïve to understand evaluation in any other way and unhelpful to do so when trying to investigate the independence of an evaluation and evaluator. In reality evaluations are probably not as independent as they are presented. They are after all commissioned to a written specification which is framed to shape a particular purpose. Evaluations can be used in the politics of decision making by policy makers at all levels of government to frame, and sometimes support, decisions.

Evidence-based practice

Evaluation research received a huge surge in its influence with the commitment of governments to evidence-based practice. The platform of What Works in social policy development and service delivery supported the development of programmes which demonstrably satisfied pre-determined criteria of effectiveness. Evaluation became the servant generating the material for decisions about what constituted evidence-based practice. Meeting requirements of evidenced-based practice unlocks funding support and shapes social policy development. Evaluation has a powerful role as a handmaiden for Government.

The focus on generating evidence to meet the What Works agenda for public services did not accord the evaluator intellectual independence or opportunity to run open enquiries. Rather it emphasises more rigid outcome monitoring, with evaluations demonstrating that the publicly funded pro-grammes have met or missed their targets. That which is evaluated is all there is, as a way of looking at problems and solutions. More open research would allow broader questioning that might even bring to the surface other understandings of the problem.

Policy and framing evaluations

Evaluations are commissioned to report on many aspects of publicly funded services, these might be pilots intended for national rollout, programme evaluations of work in progress or summative evaluations to demonstrate impact. Evaluations are asked to report on what is in place: they do not undertake blue skies thinking. Their findings are limited by the political agenda that has given rise to the initiatives they evaluate.

Evaluations can be further channelled by having prescribed lines of enquiry and methodologies which preclude wider exploration of issues and needs. In some instances evaluations are commissioned to adhere to a national evaluation framework, which allows for comparisons across a number of programmes but which neglects the peculiarities of local conditions and contexts. While this may allow description of What Works, the how and the why and the for whom can be missed. There is a 'quasi-scientific language of programme evaluation' through which 'evaluation becomes more a part of a process by which compliance with programme goals can be assured' (Taylor and Ballach, 2005: 11).[1]

Framing evaluations in these ways deprives evaluation of independence and divorces it from research and from theory building, limiting opportunities for other insightful discoveries of what may work better with certain groups.

The policy-makers' imperative

Undertaking evaluations to serve the needs of policy making can be problematic on a number of grounds.

Firstly, there may be an expectation that certain findings be discovered to support pre-determined policy development plans.

Secondly, the actual work of the evaluation, the analysis and recommendation writing can often lag behind the policy maker's timetable. Social interventions take far longer to have an effect and to evaluate than election cycles and policy direction permit. The evaluator can come under pressure to present and draw conclusions from half collected or half analysed data. This can be enormously uncomfortable for any evaluator seeking to try to run an evaluation in the public interest. The evaluator may find the policy is developed ahead of the evaluation's findings.

To try to counter such situations the development of milestones for reporting needs to be carefully considered at the time of developing the research plan and contracting to undertake the work. It is important that the policy maker's deadlines, external to the evaluation, are declared so that there can be the best dovetailing of the work and reporting of the evaluation with the needs of decision-makers. The intentions of evaluation research being, after all, to be useful and inform decision-making. If there are conflicts between a decision-maker's needs and the length of time that a meaningful evaluation will take to be completed the evaluator should draw attention to such discrepancies before the evaluation design is finalised and the contract signed. Utilisation-focused and developmental evaluation are methodologies which might help in these situations.

This may require a re-education of those commissioning an evaluation about what can constitute an evaluation.

It is however possible that a policy or personnel change may occur mid-evaluation and so the decision-making needs change. If the evaluator is forced to report on incomplete work then it must be made clear that any analysis offered is on the understanding that it is provisional. There is probably little more that an evaluator can do in these circumstances.

Thirdly, some evaluators have found that when their work is presented that 'political considerations will always provide convenient answers to awkward questions thrown up by research' (James, 1993: 113).[2] This puts the evaluator in a complicated position. What is to be done when an evaluation is dismissed because it does not meet political needs? The evaluator may own the data but not have rights to the intellectual property of their own work. They may have signed confidentiality agreements. The work is often framed and designed to meet policy requirements and is not undertaken as a more academic or independent research project. These factors can make it hard for the evaluator to present the work as research in these circumstances. The evaluator is in effect neutered and left with the uncomfortable sense of being a party to something they may feel is not right.

Finally, ministers and policy direction may change, mid-term or with changes of government. Such changes can impact evaluative work already underway. There may be no provision in the contract to allow the work to continue according to its original plan. The design may have to be adapted. Any such changes and their implications should be brought up during the reporting process.

While rolling with changes is an inevitable part of applied and policy oriented research, no evaluator wants to lose their independence and to do an inadequate job just because circumstances change. Paying attention to the likely political situations and needs of the commissioning body and taking care with the contract details may be all that can be done to try to reduce the risk of becoming a ball bearing on a political bagatelle board.

Looking at the drivers behind the commissioning and use of an evaluation

Evaluation and the politics of limited resources

Evaluations are linked to serious decisions; should programmes continue or be expanded, how should services be shaped and what are the implications for people's employment. Evaluations are often intended only to look a particular service but this singularity of focus is often impossible to maintain and the evaluator can get caught up with the personalities of those involved in development and delivery. Those making decisions do not make them purely on the basis of evaluation findings. They too can be caught up with a host of other concerns and personalities. Between commissioners and evaluators there is the potential for a multiplicity of micro-political crosscurrents. Into this mix other stakeholders' concerns and interests need to be added and so the micro-political currents are amplified. This type of noise generated around an evaluation has to be anticipated.

Evaluation as political pawn?

It is important to try to understand the political context in which an evaluation is grounded. Both the micro-politics of an organisation and the broader social and political agenda impact the organisation or programme under review. It is naïve for an evaluator to not have such awareness and it does a disservice to the evaluation. The difficulties for the evaluator in how to make use of such knowledge will come back, on many occasions, to ethics.

The commissioner's purpose

At one extreme the commissioning body may require a public interest evaluation. That is an evaluation where the investigation, analysis, reported outcomes and recommendations represent the interests of all stakeholders. At the other extreme there is partisan evaluation where the evaluator adopts the role of advisor to the decision-makers with the research and recommendations shaped to support their interests.

Whatever the style of evaluation which has been commissioned there is a strong likelihood that if external decisions about funding are aligned to the findings of the evaluation then an evaluator may come under pressure to find certain ways which would unblock future funding.

The purpose of the evaluation needs to be thought through before commissioning and its reasons should be shared with the evaluator. In turn this should be shared with those who may be the subjects of an evaluation.

Evaluating investment

A key plank in decision-making and in evaluation has become assessment of the social return on the investment and efficiencies of the intervention or service. This can affect the ways in which programmes report their successes, for example, they may down play their failures, find ways to double count numbers or err towards the lowest possible level in defining what is an intervention.

It is then hard for an evaluation to try to redefine what a project may have agreed as an indicator of success with its funder.

Considering the construction of relationships in the field

Exploiting or generating political capital

The commissioners can make use of an evaluation to make political capital. The evaluator needs to be tuned into how this is playing out. Evaluations can be hijacked and staff or beneficiaries made fearful about its possible findings and may feel the need to report positively on the work of a project lest future funding be compromised. While this anxiety to continue the work is human and understandable it does not help the evaluation. This creates an association between evaluation and fear and it will get in the way of the relationship that the evaluator can create with potential respondents.

If an evaluator suspects that there has been undue influence put on potential respondents it creates multiple difficulties in relationships with respondents, in trusting the data, in balancing any extremes of data and trusting in the relationships with those who have commissioned the work. It is a potentially uncomfortable and disconcerting experience of being manipulated, of the context being manipulated and making it hard to get a sense of reliable direction to steer by.

An evaluation can be used to justify restructuring or staff changes. This may have been a forgone conclusion. There may be an element of checking out facts through an independent evaluation but it would have been more honest to tackle such issues through effective performance management routes and a strategic review. An organisation using evaluation as a means to restructure will cement in staff minds an association of evaluation and fear.

An evaluator needs to be alive to the micro politics surrounding an evaluation. They are data.

Looking behind the evaluator's role to the person inhabiting that role

> *Research as a purely objective[3] activity removed from all aspects of politics and power is a myth no longer accepted in the research world. As early as the turn of the twentieth century, Max Weber recognised that 'the existence of a scientific problem coincides personally with . . . specifically oriented motives and values '(1904). It is now recognised that research, and therefore researchers are responsible for shaping the character of knowledge; and responsibilities associated with this knowledge production have led to growing recognition and acceptance of the need for ethical and political awareness to be a mainstream consideration in the research process. Power, politics, and ethics must now be actively managed by the researcher.*

O'Leary, 2004: 42[4]

A lengthy quotation but one arguing that the researcher is solidly grounded within their own context and that this will be brought to bear on any research which they undertake. In this section some effects of individuals are explored. Just involving a spread of stakeholders is not a sufficient antidote to the effects of the individual evaluator. An individual evaluator has to acknowledge the impacts they may make and try to explore these and account for the effects they may have.

The embodied self

The first and more obvious effects to explore are those exerted by our embodied selves. These of course work in combination with each other and will affect our world-view. Evaluator and stakeholders will impact each other through such attributes as:

Gender

Gender can be used within research relationships as in any situation. For example, some stakeholders may be made more comfortable by working with an evaluator who is female. They may find it easier to be interviewed about certain things. Other stakeholders may not want to talk to an evaluator and may use gender as a means to not be so revelatory for example, male respondents may try to patronise a female evaluator, sexualise the situation or try to turn a male evaluator into a co-conspirator. Gender will obviously impact the world-views and lived experiences of the evaluator. It will generate sets of expectations based on past experiences.

Class and social status

Class affects experiences and perceptions of stakeholder and evaluator. Discrepancies in class or social status may make an evaluator less able to collect data from stakeholders who may have had less affluent lifestyles, have less human capital or access less social capital. There may be a disconnection, lack of empathy or some type of patronage. Some evaluators may be given to polarising people, making certain attributions to people of lower social class or status than themselves. For example making assumptions about education, aspirations or the nature of their moral compass. See discussion on dichotomisation on page 58.

Race

The ethnic background and cultural experiences of the evaluator and the stakeholders will exert an impact on what might be shared within a data collection session. It may affect cues in situations of observations. Again stakeholders may not feel comfortable talking with someone from certain racial groups or feel less prepared to share certain things.

Faith

Holding certain sets of beliefs may make an evaluator more or less able to work with certain faith groups. Again, it may make the evaluator unaware of certain nuances, may make the stakeholders feel less willing to share with the evaluator. It is possible that race does not exercise an effect but awareness of differences needs to be acknowledged and potential impact explored.

Age

Age means that people are cued into certain nuances of social life, to the exclusion of others. They will have cultural references other age groups may not share. For example, younger evaluators may not be thought of as likely to understand older stakeholders. They may be perceived as less sensitive when health issues or other age-related issues are to be shared. People who are perceived as older may be seen as authority figures, people it is not possible to connect with or they may be seen as safe and able to be told things.

Education

Levels of education may give an authority to a person, for example, someone coming from a university. Evaluators with this type of background may be assumed to know about an issue, to be clever and able to see though things. The obverse of course is that they are considered 'egg-heads' and cut off from the real world. Education may be a double-edged sword. There may be fears or resentments about the educated researcher, these may manifest as deference or rejection.

Age, gender, class and social status, roles played, faith and race may all affect the ways in which stakeholders respond to the evaluator. They are qualities of the evaluator that neither evaluator nor stakeholders can do anything about. Nothing is possible beyond trying to be outwardly sensitive and appropriate and being aware of the effects which they may exert. Evaluators in developing the evaluation design might consider, with the commissioners and stakeholders, whether a more participatory design might reduce the effect of certain qualities of an evaluator. Stakeholders could be asked about any effects they think the researcher may have had on their responses. The evaluator should keep track of their own thinking about the stakeholders and the effects they think they may have had on the stakeholders. This is all data which should be taken into consideration.

It may be that in developing designs and staffing evaluation teams that there is a need to employ evaluators with a range of different attributes. For example, running focus groups with co-evaluators, one of whom may be representative of stakeholders in the group. However, there are other considerations to be made, such as levels of skill, training and so on. This is not just a simple solution to adopt unthinkingly.

The evaluator role

The evaluator role is one that will be constructed by the evaluator and those around them. It may be a role imbued with power because the evaluator may be able to make certain choices and decisions about the ways an evaluation will be conducted. The evaluator may be able to explore and get under the skin of a programme having access to stakeholders and materials. The evaluator may be sharing their perceptions with those who fund a programme. The evaluator will be presenting some conclusions and recommendations that may affect the programme and the organisation. Recognition of this power, perceptions of power and the ways in which this might exert impact needs to be acknowledged and understood.

Self-centrism and limitations of world-views

Individual researcher's values and motives will coincide with a research problem. This may be at its most obvious, in the type of issues chosen or research approaches preferred. There should be awareness of this and awareness of why the researchers' interests, limitations and preferences may not always serve an evaluation the best. For example, someone considering themselves as an expert at a certain type of research problem may become a liability because they could bring to the issue previous baggage, an intellectual short-hand or even a boredom with the issue and so fail to see a new situation for what it is. Likewise a fixity in a certain way of working may not surface the most robust or rounded data although it may have been a research design which has served well in the past.

Feminist social scientists have long drawn attention to a range of deficits in social science research methodologies and methods. An area highlighted as cause for concern is that of the self-centrism of researchers.

Self-centrism is the way in which ideas, perceptions of others, the external world and issues get sucked into a vortex of interpretation based on an individual's own lived experiences, beliefs and other limitations. The conflation of an individual's self-centrism with the role of evaluator is important. It does require a level of self-awareness and acuity on the part of the evaluator to try to identify and understand the impacts that they may have on the ways in which they collect and interpret data.

Individuals can fail to see that there are alternative realities and other ways of looking at the world than those they have. This can lead to evaluators who fail to understand the world-views of others, who bring their own values and interpretations to a situation. Evaluators may fail to distinguish who may be more representative of a particular group and so fail to hear the quieter voices.

Evaluators may apply double standards to groups of stakeholders over the same issue. Accepting a behaviour as acceptable for one group, while seeing it as unusual and penalising another group for the same behaviour endorses stereotypes within the research process. For example, being astonished at the vocational successes of a group more commonly assumed to be without aspirations.

Dichotomisation is another way that an evaluator's limited world-views may impact stakeholders, data collection and analysis. In this way people are assigned to groups at opposite ends of a manufactured spectrum and the commonality between people fails to be recognised. Again this is a way to embed prejudice and stereotypes within an evaluation. For example, dividing tenants in social housing from owners of more expensive properties and not recognising that, whatever the value of their accommodation and whatever life choices may be made, there may be concerns about more sustainable lifestyles that may be common to the two groups.

Evaluators can be insensitive to race, class, gender and so on, and to people who have different experiences to themselves. Evaluators may be insensitive to the language of different stakeholder groups that they are working with. Stakeholders may not want to be described in the terms which interventions and evaluations use. They may resist constructions of themselves as disempowered, as marginal or excluded. Evaluators may be unable to develop a shared language.

Evaluator's self-awareness is essential to understanding how their own limitation may be impacting their capacity to collect data and to make sense of it.

The use of an Evaluation Log,[5] debriefings and team meetings are essential. The Evaluation Log should be used to capture mood states and responses during data collection, analysis and evaluation meetings. This is data which will give insight into the ways in which the evaluation and the stakeholders are being approached. For example, fatigue, boredom, excitement and interest will all be powerful indicators of interest and attentiveness, as to which data collection opportunities may be up-played and which down-played.

Prior to entry into the field some attempt at trying to explore expectations of the issue and the stakeholders should be made. Writing these out may open them up to questioning and so expose some prejudices and assumptions.

The personal politics and constructions of the individual evaluators and the effects which they can exert make it all the more important to triangulate the data.

The politics of evaluation design

Choice points in any evaluation design will have a political basis. These decisions may support or challenge the socio-political constructions of certain issues, groups or interventions. For example, what is the purpose of the evaluation? What is the role of the stakeholders in framing the evaluation?

Taylor and Balloch (2005: 250) write:

> *Because the dominant discourses tend to be rooted in the managerialist/consumerist modes, service users often feel their contribution is tokenistic. Thus, there is increased questioning about involvement in evaluation – is this really to change and improve people's lives or merely to add to a body of knowledge which might even be used in an oppressive or disempowering manner?*

The reader is asked to carry in to the next chapter an awareness of the different ways in which political influences may shape an evaluation and how in turn they may be reinforced by an evaluation.

Summing up

This chapter has outlined various ways evaluations may be influenced by different political contexts, from those of broader political and policy debates, to the micro politics of an organisation or programme being evaluated. These contexts will be framing the evaluation and the evaluator's role, perhaps delimiting the scope and range of both in order to support certain policy, programme or organisational goals. The chapter has flagged ways the evaluator will impact the evaluation, through personal characteristics, beliefs and the ways in which the evaluation is designed.

Endnotes

1. Taylor, D. and Balloch, S. (2005) *The Politics of Evaluation: Participation and Policy Implementation*. Bristol, Policy Press.
2. James, M. (1993) Evaluation for Policy. In Burgess, R. Ed. *Educational Research and Evaluation: For Policy and Practice*. Lewes, Falmer Press.
3. Actually objectivity would probably not be desirable as it would mean that people were stripped of the qualities and features which make them human. Their gender and race, their past experiences and their particular interests. Taking away these elements of the people who do research would also strip away capacity for empathy, ability to relate to particular groups of people or interests in undertaking certain types of research and evaluations, working in certain types ways, for example highly participatory, or with a more positivistic methodology.
4. O'Leary, Z. (2004) *The Essential Guide to Doing Research*. London, Sage.

5. The Evaluation Log is suggested a number of times in the text. It is literally the keeping of a journal for the evaluation work. It is a place to record some of the emotions the evaluation work elicits and events of the evaluation, to record more informal observations, to record developing interpretations and observations. It is a professional but personal record and will not be used in the writing of the report, but may serve as a useful reminder of issues or as a way to check on changes of perspective.

6: Getting Down to Business

Introduction

This chapter outlines some issues which apply to many situations when an evaluation is commissioned, be this with staff internal to an organisation or external evaluators. The contracting process is a formalisation of the agreement to do the work. Given the nature of evaluations, often heavily loaded with competing expectations and concerns, it is important to make sure that what is agreed is clear, possible and negotiated. The development of a contract is more than a formal agreement, it is an opportunity to clarify what is being undertaken and how. It is an opportunity to flesh out the assumptions around the evaluation-in-mind which all parties are holding in order to develop consensus. The contract should protect all involved in the evaluation relationship and be something concrete to rely on if things go wrong in order to re-direct the work.

This chapter explores a number of areas where things might go amiss if the preliminary stages are rushed. Whilst keenness to get the work underway is understandable, it is important to generate common understandings and agreements at the outset. The chapter cannot cover every element of this contracting stage but may supply a useful line of thinking. It is important for commissioner and evaluator to stand back, think ahead and appreciate each other's points of view.

The commissioning process is in itself an interesting source of data, revealing much about the commissioner's intentions, theories in use and espoused theories. It will reveal much about the ways in which the organisation works, the nature of any partnerships and how stakeholders are thought about. It is a time when there is a need for political acuity on the part of the evaluator; without it there is a risk of it being hijacked, not least of all by a personal vision of the evaluation-in-mind. Given that the contracting process is very revelatory it is worth making use of the Evaluation Log to record feelings and impressions. The log may be a useful opportunity to reflect and to surface any concerns about this process.

The process of getting to contract should be an iterative one to ensure that there is mutual understanding of what should be happening. The chapter covers:

Commissioning

- purpose
- control of the evaluation
- organisational commitments to the evaluation and to follow-through
- commitments to stakeholders
- outputs

The evaluators

- researcher independence
- boundaries to the role
- internal evaluators

Contracting

- getting to go

Commissioning

Purpose and politics

The first thing the commissioners have to decide upon, with complete honesty, is the purpose of the evaluation. This will drive other decisions, for example, the methodology the evaluators select.

Frank discussion about purpose will also determine the success or otherwise of the evaluation. It is essential that commissioners, evaluators and stakeholders have a shared understanding of the purpose.

For example, if the commissioners want to use the evaluation as part of a package to secure further funding but do not share this with the evaluators there may be disappointments in the final report. While the evaluators cannot skew their findings, they may in the process of writing up their report, acknowledge this purpose. They might offer evidence for an external reader, demonstrating distance travelled by beneficiaries, progress in operational terms and where there are outstanding issues and what might be done to manage them. The evaluation team may have recommendations about possible expansion grounded in the findings.

Commissioning may be driven by an organisational desire to learn, by concerns about an element of provision, or it may be something dictated by contract. It may be more politically driven or partisan, seeking some ratification for a decision which has already been taken, for example, to close down a line of service. It is not the role of an evaluation to rubber stamp a decision. Robson[1] calls this 'a sin'.

An evaluator should be made aware of any such prior decisions, if the commissioners want something which is more partisan in intent. It will be up to the evaluator to decide if these are acceptable grounds on which to undertake the evaluation.

Control of the evaluation

A second key area is the degree of control that the commissioners want to exert over an evaluation, the evaluator and the outcomes. This may be a non-issue if the evaluation is styled as a participatory or public interest evaluation, if the evaluator is given independence to make decisions from start to finish or if the evaluation has some prescriptive form as part of an external contract.

However there may be a desire to exert control and this may cover a number of issues. Commissioner control may be a deal breaker. For example do the commissioners want to dictate the research questions and the tools? Is there a desire to suggest who should do the evaluation on the research team and who not? Will there be control over access to stakeholders or documents, selecting what sources of data might be used for the evaluation? Is there a desire to know which respondents said what? Is there a desire to have a power of veto over the final report and to shape the writing up process? Some of these things may not be known at the outset but it is important to try to flush out any intentions in these directions. It will make it hard for an evaluation team to work if there is a need to get approval each step along the way. It will also be difficult to gain the trust of respondents and to get frank access to information.

Issues of accountability should not be confused with control. Accountability covers matters such as progress reporting for expenditure and wanting to have sight of research tools or to have interim reports and a discussion about checking facts and interpretation.

Organisational commitments to the evaluation and to follow-through

The evaluators should ascertain the extent to which there is organisational commitment to the evaluation and to its follow-through. This is difficult at the outset and may change as the evaluation proceeds. It may also be dependent on findings or other external factors. Some questions that might be explored to test this out could include:

- what is the organisation's understanding of the role of an evaluation?
- what does the organisation expect from this evaluation?
- what does the organisation think that its role is once the report is completed?
- what resource is the organisation putting behind the evaluation?
- is there an openness to receive any findings or is there pressure to report in a particular vein?
- to what extent is the organisation a learning organisation?
- what examples are there of the ways in which the organisation works with change?
- how might the commissioners react to findings they construe as disappointing?
- what strategies are in place for working with the findings?

Discussions with the commissioners about how they would manage findings they may find challenging or disappointing, may provide some indications. Organisations need to hear and work with the positive and negative and to appreciate this both intellectually and emotionally.

There are a number of stages at which the commissioning team needs to make decisions about the type of commitment it has to an evaluation. These can include:

- opening the ways for the evaluators to access various stakeholders
- making access possible to organisational and programme documentation and records
- making a budget available to cover realistic evaluation costs: these may include incentivising participation, covering stakeholder costs, making work time available for staff and volunteers
- working within a realistic time frame for the evaluation and therefore the budget for the evaluation
- making time for interim reporting and discussion of emergent issues
- sharing development plans with the evaluation team and being open about the ways in which the evaluation fits into development plans

Those commissioning the evaluation need to think about the degree to which they want to work with the outcomes of the evaluation:

- hearing what a variety of stakeholders say about what is being done or offered and acting on any concerns and suggestions which surface
- managing any findings which initially they would have considered contrary to their operation or interests
- determining what role others in the organisation may have for working with the findings of the evaluation
- following up any recommendations from the evaluation team even if, after consideration, the decision is to reject them
- developing a strategy to work with identified changes

A lack of will to listen to that which may be initially unpalatable and a lack of will to explore recommendations will leave an evaluation as an 'unactioned' report. This could alienate staff and clients from further activities involving evaluations and self-assessment, by generating a sense that there is little organisational regard for the concerns and opinions of staff and other stakeholders.

Personalities

The commissioning body needs to think carefully about the very senior managers in the organisation, chief executives, programme directors and others who may have a vested interest in the work and the evaluation. There are multiple opportunities for overly invested staff to feel offended at an evaluation. This may affect the course of the evaluation and the commitment of the organisation to work with the findings and explore the recommendations from the evaluation. This would be to miss opportunities for development and would be likely to alienate some staff and other stakeholders who contributed their time to the evaluation.

Sharing and exploring broader information sets

Some types of evaluation, those which are more formative or concerned to help in the development of business strategies, may provide some broader contextual information as part of the evaluation. This could include information on other competition in the area, projects with which partnerships or alliances might be developed, and any emerging legislation or regulations likely to exert an impact on changes to funding streams and other such impact-exerting developments. This means that the organisation has to be in tune with its context and not in denial about the ways in which changes in its context might impact it.

Previous in-house, informal or formal evaluations need to be shared with the evaluation team. These may offer a baseline to the evaluation and allow for the development of a more coherent story. For example, to trace operational developments and responses to earlier comments about operational shortfalls, to help explain why certain developments were undertaken and to show with evidence how a programme has listened to earlier comment.

Commitments to stakeholders

In moving towards commissioning an evaluation thought needs to be given to the range of stakeholders to be involved and how they are to be involved. There needs to be agreement between what the evaluation team considers will give the best results and the commitment the organisation can make, for example, to sharing the findings with the stakeholders or the extent of the organisation's interest in what the broader stakeholder groups might think of the work under review.

There may be no choice if the evaluation design is to some degree determined by an external funder. Assuming there is choice for the commissioning team then issues such as the extent of involvement of stakeholders in design, the degree to which stakeholders are asked to provide data or review the emerging findings, will need to be agreed. These decisions will have budgetary and time considerations.

Protections to stakeholders

This involves thinking about the ways the evaluators will be able to approach people for their experiences as part of data collection.

There may be formal mechanisms in place that protect people. For example, an Internal Review Board or other ethics committee, within the organisation or the authority itself. Where vulnerable people are concerned there are most likely to be external checks on organisations undertaking their own evaluations, for example additional review boards in areas of health and education.

Collection and use of personal information will need to conform to the Data Protection Act[2] and there will need to be conformation to policies about working with vulnerable adults, young people and to organisational requirements for security in prisons, young offender institutes and bail hostels. There will also need to be conformity to policies for child protection.

The commissioning team may also want to consider how it wants to ensure that any stakeholders contributing to the evaluation are protected. This may include agreements with the evaluators about the confidentiality and anonymity of the data collected and its presentation in reports and other project outputs.

The commissioners may agree that they have no rights to privileged information and will not know who said what. It is likely that the evaluators will be working to their own professional guidelines as evaluators and as social scientists[3] and it would be an expectation that they would naturally write into any of their own contracts clauses about anonymity and confidentiality.

Anonymity and confidentiality will be particular issues to negotiate when an evaluation is small-scale and it would be easy to identify particular people. This is also an issue where organisations and partnerships offer a range of boutique style services.

Internal evaluations will have a number of elements to explore in terms of anonymity and confidentiality. For example staff may be especially concerned about talking to colleagues who are their peers about their experiences of a programme, the people they work with or their perceptions of the organisation and its support to them. Clients may be concerned about talking to another staff member. There may be concerns about reprisals, who will have access to what they say, giving another staff member in the evaluation role privileged access to their thoughts and concerns, and about inadvertent leakage of information across the evaluator-participant boundary.

Outputs

The outputs need thinking through so evaluation effort and resources serve as many needs as possible and these can be specified at the point of contracting. The evaluators will need to know if, for example, they have to write a number of summaries for different audiences as well as a final report. This may involve them in taking photos during the fieldwork for some types of report and thinking about graphic representations of some of their findings. This has cost and time implications and needs to be known up front. The evaluators may also have other ideas for sharing the results of the evaluation if they know that there are different audiences to be appraised of the work. For example there may be short reports and summaries for policy makers and other agencies, service users and general release, along with a report for the organisation.

The outputs will differ from simple text reports if for example participatory video[4] making is one of the research methods or if the service users are themselves involved in the collection and analysis of the data. More participatory outputs have time and financial considerations.

Thinking carefully about outputs before contracting may drive choice of methods, the evaluators and the types of skills they bring. It will impact on costs and so setting a realistic budget. It will also be important for the evaluators to know what they can offer to those whom they approach for their involvement.

The evaluators

Researcher independence

Having an appropriate fit between evaluator, organisation and project is essential for the quality of the work and outputs and for the quality and smoothness of the relationship. Open discussion about issues such as those outlined above will help in the process of determining if the commissioner-evaluator relationship is a viable one. This needs to be worked through even if the evaluator is an internal one. Internal evaluations are under special pressures, collecting data from colleagues, other familiar stakeholders and beneficiaries.

While it is tempting for evaluators to chase a contract themselves, for the sake of getting in work and revenue, it is important to think about the ways in which the work:

- sits within their broader portfolio of interest and expertise
- supports any future plan for development of particular work streams
- resonates with the types of work which they may prefer ideologically to undertake

While in difficult economic times these may seem less helpful observations they are ones which underpin a more effective working relationship.

Commissioners may likewise wish to simply 'get on with' the evaluation. There may be pressures because of an external contract, an up-coming funding round or concerns about trying to balance service provision and make resources stretch appropriately in difficult times.

Standing back to consider what is on the table is important for both sides.

Elements for evaluators to consider might include a list such as the following:

- the ways in which an evaluator may prefer to work with stakeholders
- the extent of interest in more summative evaluations if this is what is on the table
- particular expertise in, for example, narrative and qualitative research as opposed to quantitative work
- the types of pressures which can be anticipated in a particular evaluation and if these can be managed
- the substantive area of enquiry and if there is any expertise in this

Unless the evaluators are prepared to buy into an explicitly delineated evaluation or one explicitly politically driven there will be questions about professional independence. This might be in relation to issues such as:

- the development of the evaluation design
- access to stakeholders at various levels of the system
- contextual data, including if needed, financial data
- having agreed reporting periods and tasks
- exercising judgment about pursuing particular lines of enquiry
- adding other lines of enquiry
- confidentiality of the data: data being held by the evaluation team and only discussed within that team
- anonymity of the data in presentations
- not being pressurised to breach any confidentiality should difficult issues emerge
- the final report covering the key items agreed in the research design
- not being pressurised into writing a report which has the findings and analysis which the commissioning team would have preferred

Boundaries to the role

Part of independence includes a prior negotiation of boundaries. This may be open to subsequent negotiation but members of the evaluation team should not find themselves forced into taking up other roles. These could include:

- during the evaluation counselling the staff or chief executive, taking on consultative roles, providing coaching, providing mentoring, writing resources or re-shaping a failing project
- writing several versions of the evaluation findings or undertaking presentations if this had not been previously agreed
- writing sanitised versions of the evaluation findings to support organisational needs which compromise the integrity of the evaluation
- at the close of the evaluation moving from evaluative roles into consultant roles to develop and implement some of the recommendations from the evaluation. This is a role-shift which would

preclude further evaluative work and it may lead to a limitation in the ways options or recommendations could be developed in the final report

If a developmental evaluation methodology were adopted then there would be movement between evaluation and organisational development roles. But this would have been previously negotiated.

All evaluators need to be alive to the political context in which they are working and to be able to manage themselves, their team and the project within political and cultural contexts. To fail to be aware of such is likely to lead to problems.

All evaluators should be clear about the terms of the contract, and work to that. While it is for their protection, for example, to prevent having to take on other work or to adopt new roles, it is also for the commissioning team, so that they do not end up with an evaluation which goes off along a tangent that may be of research interest but does not meet organisational need. Working to an agreed contract with professional standards of ethics should enable evaluators to keep sources of information confidential and not come under pressure to write reports which are inappropriately skewed.

Internal evaluators

Some of the benefits of using internal evaluators include being less costly than external evaluators. Also they often take less time to become familiar with that which is being evaluated and be more attuned to the operating culture of the parent organisation and so be more liable to generate suggestions which fit well within the existing culture. Internal evaluation could be seen as a positive because it may cause fewer ripples than bringing in an outsider.

Internal evaluation could be considered a benefit in that it would be developing capacity, which represents an important step along the road to developing internal competency for evaluation.

Framing internal assessments can be useful in building consensus for the evaluation and so a commitment about what might be resourced and supported following the evaluation (Wolf, 1999).[5]

However there are a number of issues in employing internal evaluators for both the organisation and for those employed to undertake the work.

Internal evaluators, if not specifically employed to do this work, may need to be trained to undertake the work and have an understanding of what evaluation research is, an awareness of the processes and the required skill sets. Asking someone to bolt evaluation onto an existing role or taking them off a task to undertake the evaluation does not respect the individual, the value of the task which is being undertaken or those who will be impacted by the evaluation and its outcomes.

Internal evaluators need to be very careful about their independence and boundary management. They will face difficult times if those commissioning the work at one point promised a free-rein and then decide to draw this in. Internal evaluators may face problems in getting colleagues and service users to talk openly. Potential respondents may be fearful of reprisals and being reported to management. If internal evaluators are put under pressure to share sources this will compromise not only the evaluation but will open up the larger issue of trust within the organisation and damage its psychological contract.[6]

Boundary management may also be an issue in terms of ensuring that they have the time and the resources to complete the work. They should not be diverted to other tasks, be asked to implement early findings or face the prospect that the evaluation is aborted part-way through.

Internal evaluators do need to ensure that they are fully informed of the reasons for the evaluation and that they have access to the data they need to do the work. This may be hard because there may be issues in trying to interview stakeholders with higher status than themselves. There may be issues for internal evaluators in accessing material that may be considered sensitive such as financial information, staff salaries and qualifications. There may be difficulties in accessing organisational development plans. There may be concerns in sharing this type of data with an internal evaluator for fear that confidences could be breached.

An internal evaluator will need some assurance about their own role within the organisation if the evaluation offers findings which some consider difficult to manage. They will need to remain neutral and independent within situations where they are party to much privileged information. They may have to manage conflicts of interest and loyalty with their colleagues, who may want to describe that which is being evaluated in the best or worst light.

Internal evaluators may have to revert to a role without such access to the privileged information they had collected or to a role without any part in implementing their findings. This can be hard.

Internal evaluators have to manage the issues of speaking the same organisational and operational languages as their colleagues, and yet they must try not to make assumptions about common understanding and shared meanings.[7] They need to pretend they have outsider status and encourage colleagues to spell out what they understand to be the situation. This is hard. It takes more time and it immediately severs some possible routes to ready rapport.

The internal evaluator may like to negotiate for some external consultancy to help support the framing of the evaluation, questions, design and approaches. They may want to have some external supervision to help them manage field issues or what they may experience as conflicts of interest, their own feelings about wanting to represent the work in the best or worst light or feelings of being torn between colleagues and the drivers of the evaluation. There may be ethical or political issues which need to be discussed. The internal evaluator may want to explore field issues about access, confidentiality or what can be done with certain sorts of privileged information. While just sitting with concerns and issues could allow for distortions and lack of perspective and perhaps escalating an issue or failing to see relevance.

The role of internal evaluator can be one of being the filling in the sandwich and so a hard role to play. It has a power attached to it and will attract any number of prejudices, perceptions and projections.

Contracting

Getting to go

The contract should be in place before work begins. The actual elements of the contract will depend on the organisations involved. Some considerations for contract headings follow below, but there should also be the inclusion of some of the issues rehearsed above which have a bearing on the complex issues of ethics, boundaries, purpose and independence. Elements which may not be standard in contracts but which might be worth considering include some of the following.

Ownership of the data and the report

Is there an opportunity for the evaluator to produce this material as a research report, to talk or write about the work? Can any learning from the work be used in other circumstances such as at a conference or developed into a learning resource or tool kit?

If the commissioning body is prepared to share the learning from the evaluation, then thought about possible products and ways to disseminate the information should be included in the contract. There are many instances when the work being evaluated may have a commercial value and the commissioning body should consider how it wants to protect its interests.

If the body undertaking the evaluation is an academic body or other research based organisation there is a likelihood that they would wish to publish from the work. Publication and intellectual ownership of various elements of the work need to be cleared up in advance.

Extent of support from the organisation

This usually includes descriptions of access to sources of data and reports and in-kind support like premises on which to conduct the research. If there are any areas of information the evaluator cannot access, for example financial data, this should be included in the contract. If the commissioning organisation is going to supply data about beneficaries' contact details or run events to bring stakeholders together this should be specified.

Harder to reach groups

These are often some of the beneficiaries of interventions. For some groups mobile phone numbers and last known addresses can be out of date very quickly. If there is an expectation that a certain number of stakeholders from such groups be surveyed or interviewed and this turns out later not to be possible then alternatives need to be considered in the risk assessment element of the contract. The evaluator should not be penalised for something beyond their control.

Confidentiality

This clause would work in several directions. The evaluation team should know if they can offer assurances to stakeholders about the confidentiality of the data. If ownership of the data is the research team's, then decisions should be taken about how long the data should be kept and where. This should be in the contract.

Budget

A full budget should be agreed ahead of starting. This may include some contingencies if additional work is needed or some element of the contingency planning has to be enacted. The budget should be comprehensive including, if appropriate, incentives for stakeholders and funds for stakeholder training.

Reporting and accountability

The cycle of reporting, form of reports and areas to be covered should be specified in the contract. This should follow the agreed research design and not be subject to changes because of the organisation's changing needs.

Outputs

The various outputs should be specified in as much detail as possible without closing down options for the evaluation team in advance. The commissioning body should not make assumptions that more reports would be written or different forms of the data be produced if this has not been agreed in advance of the work starting.

Timescale

This needs to be realistic. It is important that both evaluator and the commissioning body develop a mutual appreciation of preliminary but essential activities like contacting stakeholders to appraise them of the evaluation, undertaking any stakeholder training and the time demands of certain types of fieldwork. It is essential that any external deadlines impacting data collection, analysis and reporting are shared ahead of starting the work.

It is essential that the evaluators are made aware of any events that may impact their work, for example programme closures, staff training, anticipated changes of personnel or changes to the programme.

A realistic methodology and design has to be committed to and this may mean disabusing commissioners of any unrealistic ideas they may hold. There is no point in committing to an impossible timetable and unrealistic design to please commissioners and then having to try to unpick the arrangement or rush the task.

Risk assessment

The risk assessment should be included in the contract. This should have been worked through and contingencies agreed between evaluator and commissioning body. For example what happens if a certain type of data cannot be collected.

The contract protects these early stages of decision-making, defines roles, boundaries and expectations. It should supportively help the evaluation so that the work can be undertaken without difficulties.

Summing up

Without negotiating an intelligent and comprehensive contract the evaluation will be likely to be doomed from the outset. Those commissioning have an obligation to undertake some soul searching to ensure they are actually commissioning an evaluation and not trying to buy a rubber-stamping of pre-made decisions. They need to be fully cognisant of the processes involved in an evaluation, to know the information has to be readily available and that there is an obligation to hear both good and less good comments about services that are offered. The commissioners need to have thought their way into the process and to the conclusion of the process, and to be aware of how they might work with the reports and other outputs from the evaluation.

For evaluators it is important that, rather than simply chase a contract, they consider, before getting embroiled in the work, how viable the proposed work is, whether there are immediate alerts about important issues such as the control a commissioner wants to exert.

Evaluators may want to consider how the proposed work fits with a developing portfolio of work and expertise. How the proposed work aligns with their existing and developing skills sets and methodological interests.

For internal evaluators there are a number of additional issues to consider and from the outset it is important to pay attention to these in order not to be put at risk. These include for example, their own and the organisation's capacity for boundary management, their trust in assurances offered by the organisation about the confidentiality of data, the nature of the organisation and how it will manage any difficult findings. There may be issues for internal evaluators in being able to undertake the evaluation role and if necessary reverting to playing other roles within the organisation after the evaluation.

The key message of the chapter is the importance of agreeing the rules of engagement before embarking on the evaluation.

Endnotes

1. Robson, C. (2000) *Small Scale Evaluation*. London, Sage.
2. Data Protection Act (UK) 1998, http://www.legislation.gov.uk/ukpga/1998/29/contents
3. Examples of such can be found at UK Evaluation Society, http://www.evaluation.org.uk/resources/guidelines.aspx; American Evaluation Association, http://www.eval.org/gptraining/gptrainingoverview.asp
4. A description and several other participatory methods in Squirrell, G. (2011) *Engagement in Action*. Lyme Regis, Russell House Publishing.

5. Wolf, T. (1999) *Managing a Non-profit Organisation in the 21st Century.* 3rd edn. New York, Simon and Schuster.

6. Armstrong, M. (2009) *Human Resource Management Practice.* 11th edn. London, Kogan Page.

7. Powney, J. (1988) Structured Eavesdropping. *Research Intelligence*, 28, 3–4.

7: Designing an Evaluation

Introduction

Design is the process that takes evaluation from the initial question areas through the process of data collection, and then on to analysis and the generation of outputs. This chapter takes apart the black box of design. It explores some of the decisions to be taken and their implications. There are several factors which may impact the design process and take some of the control from the evaluator. These include:

- the requirements of the commissioning body, for example in terms of approach or outputs
- constraints because the tender for the evaluation specifies a particular methodology and the means of data collection. Some may even specify the types of questions to be included in interviews or questionnaires and the nature and numbers of different types of respondents
- audit and evaluation systems which have been pre-defined as part of the funder's grant requirements
- the development of interventions with outcome monitoring and evaluation designs written into the project plan. Later stage evaluations will need be based on previous outcome monitoring and evaluation data and the questions formulated at an earlier stage in the project's life about impact and success

There are other elements that may impact the design which are more circumstantial. Some may be clear at the outset, such as resource constraints, others may emerge such as difficulties in getting ethics clearance or failure to access certain stakeholder groups. Some of these are explored in the course of the chapter, including:

- purpose
- design questions
- matching methodologies and purpose
- scoping stakeholders
- matching methodology, methods and sample respondents to evaluation questions and intentions
- timetabling and resource planning
- risk assessment
- initial stages
- the field work or data collection phase
- data analysis

Purpose

The crucial element for commissioners to establish is the purpose of the evaluation. A quick reminder of some of the ground covered in Chapter 1:

- is the evaluation intended for development?
- is the intention to make operational improvements to an intervention?
- is it a summative evaluation?
- is there a desire to contribute generalisable findings or other types of knowledge?
- is the evaluation exploratory?
- is it intended to support or endorse certain ideas?

- is the evaluation of public interest?
- it there a desire to develop democratic and participatory approaches?
- is there a desire to involve stakeholders in the design and execution of the evaluation and working with its findings?
- what roles is it intended stakeholders' interests might play and how might these be met?

The immediate concern of any evaluation team must be to clarify the purpose: fuzziness of purpose is a key element in the 'failure' of an evaluation. This may mean that the evaluation is not properly executed or that the commissioners are disappointed in the findings.

Expectations and pre-existing data

Exploration of expectations is an essential piece of work to be undertaken with the commissioners and those stakeholders who receive and may implement the evaluation. There may also be a need to explore expectations and clarify the expressed purpose with a wider range of stakeholders, to dispel concerns and manage expectations.

It is important to clarify, if there has been prior evaluation, how the proposed evaluation is intended to link with those findings. This is a useful exercise because it flushes out more about the expectations of the commissioners: whether they valued or disliked the earlier evaluation and why this may be so. This discussion will generate important data for defining purposes and expectations. A previous evaluation may also have highlighted strengths, weaknesses, developmental or contentious points or made recommendations. These are to some extent a baseline and should be taken into account in the process of data collection and reporting.

Another area to explore is the existence and use of various types of management information. This is useful data in its own right. For example in evaluating an intervention there may be management information on:

- throughput of clients
- retention of clients
- drop out
- recruitment and no shows
- completion
- outputs, for example qualifications gained by participants
- actual and budgeted costs, to be explored for any drift and to be explored for costs per head, modelling return on investment and so on
- community support
- staffing levels, turnover, costs, qualifications, and complaints

Other types of intervention will involve other types of management information. The existence of such information and the uses to which it has been put provides useful data about what the project values, how it underpins its decision-making processes and how it defines its successes.

Design questions

From purpose there is a need to get to the evaluation issues and question. This may come directly from the stated aim of the programme or organisation, from its mission statement. It is possible that there is no clear mission statement or set of objectives. It may be that there are particular elements of work the commissioner wants explored. In shaping the research areas it is important to understand the use of the evaluation. There should be no difficulties in focused evaluation working from a utilisation-focused approach.

Matching methodologies and purpose

The commissioners' and evaluators' preferences for methodologies and methods should not drive the design of the evaluation. The methodology and methods should be appropriate to the purpose of the evaluation and the research questions. It is possible that practical constraints need to be taken into account. For example, time, reporting deadlines or budgets, may make what would have been an obvious candidate for a participatory evaluation into a more focused and partial utilisation-focused evaluation with a very limited use of some more creative methodologies to engage harder to reach stakeholders.

The evaluator should spend some time thinking through the implications of selecting the right methodology and methods. They will influence the data that can be collected and this will affect what the evaluator can report upon. 'It is worth remembering that what we observe is not nature itself, but nature exposed to our method of questioning'[1]

Allied to thinking about how to answer the questions and to meet the purpose is that of establishing who might provide the data. Decisions about informants will drive the methods.

Scoping stakeholders

There are two stages in this part of the design process. First is that of taking a step back and considering all the possible stakeholders in relation to the evaluation topic. Diagramming this out may be a useful route: considering those closest to the issue and then working further out through staff, beneficiaries, carers, community, local authorities, society at large and so on.

This is an opportunity to think a little more laterally about the evaluation. Whilst considering methodology and methods it is worthwhile also to review whether there are any less obvious stakeholders whom it might be useful to approach, what they might offer the evaluation and how their data might be sought. It is useful to answer questions about stakeholders and stakeholder relationships such as:

- are there any stakeholders who might act as substitutes for other stakeholders in the data collection?
- what are the relationships between the stakeholders and the evaluation topic?
- what are the relationships between the stakeholders?
- how might these relationships affect willingness to be involved with the evaluation?
- how might these relationships affect the type of data which may be collected?
- does one group exercise an influence over another and how might this be taken into account?

Thinking about these types of questions may help at a later stage when approaching stakeholders for their involvement. For example, some stakeholders might encourage others to be involved or may help in the up-take of the findings.

Understanding the spread of stakeholders is especially important if evaluation is participatory. It ensures that all groups with some type of stake are invited to become involved.

Finally the evaluator should consider the broad spread of stakeholders and thus avoid certain stakeholder voices becoming too dominant. It helps to keep some type of balance in thinking about collecting data.

The next step is that of narrowing down the stakeholders to be approached as the methodology, methods and any practical considerations are taken into account. The list should relate to the evaluation questions and how best to answer them. Desired stakeholders should not be removed just because they may be too difficult to contact.

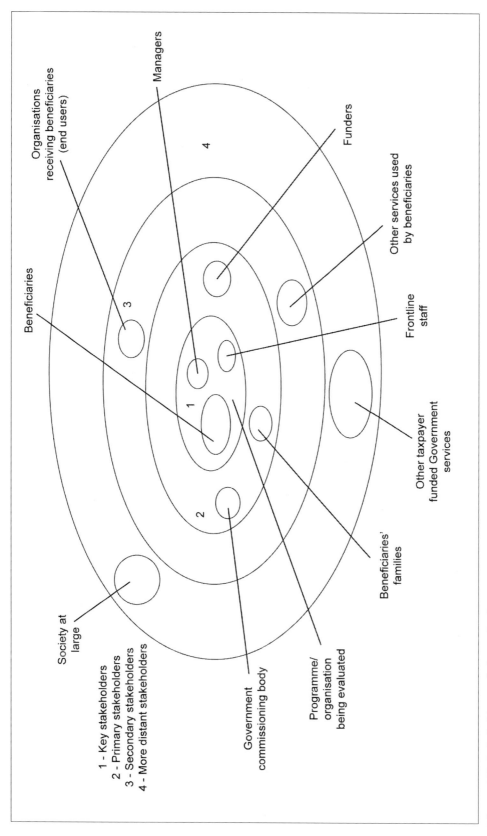

Diagram 18: Stakeholders and Rings of Influence

Managers

Organisations receiving beneficiaries (end users)

Funders

Other services used by beneficiaries

Beneficiaries

4

3

Frontline staff

1

2

Other taxpayer funded Government services

Society at large

Beneficiaries' families

Government commissioning body

Programme/ organisation being evaluated

1 - Key stakeholders
2 - Primary stakeholders
3 - Secondary stakeholders
4 - More distant stakeholders

Given this refined list of stakeholders it is important to discover if there are any issues relating to any particular groups, for example ethical, time or resource budgeting issues. Consider age, any vulnerabilities or dependencies of the stakeholders and how this might affect:

- selection of methods and the development of research tools
- the types of evaluators who might best work with these stakeholders
- any time implications for getting ethical approvals
- issues for the risk assessment process
- any time or other resource issues, for example, the need to incentivise involvement, the need to run more group activities or the need to take activities to stakeholders

The commissioners may have views about certain stakeholder groups being involved or excluded. It is important to explore their views and the implications for the research design. In such discussions there may be valuable field insights. These should be captured in the Evaluation Log.

Matching methodology, methods and sample respondents to evaluation questions and intentions

The design process now has a number of key elements under wraps:

- purpose
- a set of evaluation questions to answer
- a general strategy, the methodology
- stakeholders to be involved as informants

Decisions are needed on some of the finer details of the design methods and sample size.

Methods

Within the broader approach which is being adopted, what options are there in terms of methods which might be used for each stakeholder group to help get the types of data needed to satisfy the evaluation questions? There is a discussion of methods in Chapters 8 and 9. For example, a decision may have been taken to undertake a single point quantitative post-intervention study using a survey to collect data from people who had experienced the intervention and from a naturally occurring quasi-control group. Thinking about the likelihood of responses, especially from the group which had not experienced the intervention, it may be decided that a short face-to-face survey would be most likely to generate the sufficiency of data that was needed, as it would be more likely that people would reply. As in this example it is important to think about the evaluation from others' points of view, what can be done to make participation more interesting and likely? The choice of methods may differ across stakeholder groups, the information sought may be the same, but the methods need to be geared to stimulating responses. There is, as with choice of methodology, no reason to get trapped into one way of thinking.

Similarly in considering tools for data collection there is no reason to exclude those already available and which have been proven to work. For example, there is a survey tool for measuring criminal attitudes and behaviours, there are standardised tests to measure literacy, depression and levels of self-esteem. Such tools have already been subject to tests for their reliability and validity. They may have advantages in that they may be used in other evaluations and so may make any comparative work or discussions about different interventions easier. Obviously pre-made inventories and tools have to be fit for your evaluative purpose: they may have been designed for your stakeholder group, for example.

If there is a decision to undertake interviews, it is worth thinking about other qualitative methods which may be more attractive to potential respondents for example story-telling or testimonials.

All methods will generate data which has to be analysed, through the development of categories or units for analysis. Qualitative data of many types can be coded and can therefore yield some material for quantitative analysis. It is important to think around the possibilities of various types of data and match the method to the purpose of the data collection and not be driven by preconceptions.

Aside from a range of stakeholders there may be other data sources. Management information was mentioned above, but there may be other project documentation and wider materials such as policy documents and research literature, HM Inspection reports and works produced by other research institutions or organisations. Chapter 9 considers working with documentary analysis. But again, just because this may not be obvious it is not a reason to exclude it from consideration of what methods may be useful.

The numbers of respondents

The numbers of respondents needed for any method to be reliable will be driven by the evaluation questions, the numbers involved in the intervention or project being evaluated and the selected research method. For example, if there is a decision to plump for very deep data rich methods then ethnographic, observation, case study and narrative approaches will not permit large sample sizes. The point at issue here is that this will not permit any generalisations.

Working with data for statistical analysis there will be a need for larger sample sizes. For example, to generate data for statistical analysis of the most basic kind a minimum of 30 respondents per group is needed. As ambitions grow to undertake analysis of several variables, so the sample size must increase, to include a minimum of 25 respondents per subdivision; for multivariate analysis, the analysis of simultaneous relationships among several variables there will need to be a minimum of 10 cases for each variable.

The confidence level, how sure that the finding is more than just coincidence, will be dictated by sample size; this sampling needs to be explored with the help of a reliable text on statistical analysis. There are clear rules to follow.

Sampling amongst stakeholders may not be an issue in, for example, a small numbers evaluation. There may be only one head of learning programmes or one housing manager. In order to have their perspectives both as managers and as leading certain functional fields they have to be involved in the data collection. Where there may be many people passing through a programme the group may be stratified according to variables which the evaluation wants to test against, for example, gender, age or previous highest levels of achievement.

Sampling especially for larger groups and for quantitative surveys may be undertaken as follows:

- *simple random sampling*: every person in the population group is considered equally likely of being sampled, so say 50 are needed, they will be selected from a list at random
- *systematic sampling* would be to take say every 10th person on a list
- *stratified sampling* would be to break the total population down by the variables which are of interest and then to sample from those groups. Breaking the whole population down in this way will show if there are sufficient in each group in order to be able to explore those variables

Other types of sampling include *volunteer sampling*, but this potentially affects the data, as the respondents may be especially for or against what is being evaluated. Other options might include *hand-picked samples* if the evaluator wants to get data from certain groups amongst a whole. This however skews the data.

There are fewer issues about sampling in evaluation than in other types of social research because what is being evaluated is something which is known, for example people have either been part of an intervention or not. There should in most cases be no reason for the researcher to try to generate *convenience samples* or *snowball samples*, which will again skew the results.

Is it possible?

It is important to question the realism of the developing design at this point:

- will the methodology, the proposed methods and suggested tools, the stakeholders to be sampled and the sample sizes give robust data sets?
- can data be triangulated? (see p 83 for an explanation)
- will there be a sufficiency of data to address the evaluation purpose and questions?
- will there be a sufficiency of data to allow for generalisability?

Having got this far the next sets of questions are more practically motivated. They include timetabling, resource needs, costs and risk assessments.

Timetabling and resource planning

Chapter 9 offers several process steps for working with timetabling, based on Gantt Charting, estimating time and resources needed for an evaluation. Most organisations have a costing framework and formula for overheads. Some charities and funders allow for overheads at an agreed rate, others do not.

Realistic costing of time and personnel is the only sensible route. There is no point in attempting to get work by promising the impossible at an impossibly low price. Commissioners will see through it, be concerned about the quality of the work, the experience of those putting in the tender and the likelihood of completion. Discussion of a couple of different versions of the proposal would be a more professional route to walk. One version being the preferred methodology and extent of the sampling, and a scaled down version if funding is more of an issue. It is worthwhile finding out about funding before submitting a proposal.

Ensure that there are staged payments for the work, perhaps attached to agreed project milestones.

Risk assessment

It is important to include risk assessment in the design process with so many uncontrollable variables, contractual obligations, opportunities for reputational risk and financial exposure. Some contracts will require its inclusion.

Assessing risk is done in four stages, by:

1. Identifying risks. These may be:
   - *specific threats* which are known about
   - *possible sources of risk*, which are not known but which might impact the evaluation
2. Quantifying which threats or uncertainties pose what type of risk, by size of impact and probability of occurrence.
3. Analysing the information to determine which are the potential problems for this specific project and their likely impact on the project. List those which are finally chosen.
4. From the list in Step 3 devise responses and action plans to deal with them.

Common risks in an evaluation could include:

- various reasons for time delays. Consider some means to manage delays
- ethics approval delayed or withheld. Consider an alternative plan for data capture if this happens and the strength of this alternative, in order to answer the evaluation questions

- failure to get access to various stakeholders. Are there other gatekeepers who might be approached? Would incentives help and what might these be? How might participation be made easier or more attractive? e.g. take events to the respondents so they don't have to travel or have more creative data collection instead of administering a questionnaire
- staffing issues, such as sickness, staff leaving or not being able to recruit certain types of staff expertise. Consider who else might do the work for example, from a partner organisation or have a list of substitute staff
- loss of data. Think about steps to back up electronic data and have alternative off-site storage; pay attention to the data protection act 1998. Think about ways to copy other forms of data

There may be extraordinary risks but these need to be considered. For example:

- a national rail strike or similar which makes getting to sites for data collection difficult
- employing interns who prove not to have the skill levels or skills set which had been presumed
- the failure to recruit participant evaluators

Working on risk assessments will help develop a realistic project plan in terms of time and budget. Some risks and contingency costs might be factored in and some additional time might be allowed, for example if the there is failure to access respondents or there is a hold up with ethical approval.

Consider where risks might be shared or the commissioner might be able to help, for example, supplying names and contact details of all past programme participants.

If there are some risks for which an antidote cannot be found, consider an alternative which might still support the evaluation questions. For example, if some respondents cannot be found, consider getting data from other sources, for example staff and participant records. Consider how data might be collected from similar projects or through a literature review to help address some elements of evaluation questions. The risk assessment may well be a formal part of a contract, so the action plans and contingency plans need to be realistic.

Initial stages

There are a number of early steps which get the evaluation from design stages to becoming operational, these include:

- *designing the evaluation tools.* These need to be piloted with people similar to those from whom data will be sought. There are issues in working with stakeholders before ethical clearances have been secured. The tools which are to be used often need to be submitted to win ethical clearance. There is something of a chicken and egg problem here, as until the tools are piloted it cannot be fully confirmed that these are the final tools
- *selecting any pre-existing tools* which will help create the data pool which is needed. These might include a variety of instruments to measure states of well-being or attitudes, they need to be suitable for the evaluation questions and the stakeholders
- *ethical clearances.* These have to be completed and submitted as soon as it is known that the work is to go ahead. This can take time
- *describing and promoting the work to stakeholders* who may have an interest in engaging with the research, for example organisations working in a similar substantive area
- *searching for literature and data which may provide a useful context* for the evaluation
- *approaching stakeholders to ask permission to undertake the fieldwork.* The request will have to be provisional on ethics clearances

- *briefing and training the evaluation team*
- *locating and booking venues for the fieldwork* once it has been given approval

The fieldwork or data collection phase

Fieldwork must not be started before there are ethical clearances, no matter what the timetabling constraints might be. Other tasks might be undertaken if there are fieldwork delays, such as literature reviews or desk analysis.

There should be effective time budgeting for the fieldwork stage. It inevitably takes longer than it may seem that it should. Entry to certain stakeholders groups may need to be negotiated; events may need to be created and people invited, for example focus groups or activities such as story telling. Data flow should be monitored to check if certain data sets are coming in light and if so additional sources of data are needed.

The evaluation team will need to be supported during this phase. They need to have opportunities to explore field issues, for example, with gaining access or hearing disturbing data. There may be issues to explore in data analysis, such as the development of coding trees or technical difficulties in managing a statistical package used for analysis.

It is essential that the team has opportunities to share insights into the data and their concerns. It is important to take advantage of a team's potential for a diversity of views and interpretations as this keeps the evaluation strong. It is important to ensure that there is a common standard for quality of the data. It is important that any field issues are resolved, or at least attempts are made to resolve them before they become larger issues.

Data analysis

Data analysis is discussed in the following chapters. When thinking about design allow for some early data analysis to get a feel for the emerging findings. This might be at a very early or pilot stage to check that tools do generate the type of data needed to address the evaluation questions. Early reviews are also opportunities to ensure that there is parity of understanding and quality of work across the research team.

Interim analysis of data may generate some emerging categories that might be further tested within the field. This is only possible with certain designs. Interim data review may also ensure that all stakeholder categories have a reasonable number of respondents. It may be that a booster sample needs to be arranged if types and numbers of respondents are not representative.

There should be sufficient time allowed for data analysis and write up. The findings and recommendations should not be rushed. The consequences of the use of an evaluation can be serious: programme expansion, the shutting down of a service, remodelling provision to better support service users' needs or changes to employment.

Summing up

This chapter has explored evaluation design, where there needs to be thoughtful and creative judgment. Designing what is intended to be an effective evaluation is to do something which needs to follow logic and some rules, but it is also an opportunity to exercise choice, to be alive to the various implications of those choices and to be prepared, in some cases, to use creativity in order to undertake a research programme which generates the best quality and fullest data.

The design process is often fascinating and enjoyable. It is a process of informed planning which can also generate data. For example, it is the opportunity to model what might happen if particular stakeholders are excluded from the data collection; it is a chance to explore with the commissioners their definitions of programme success and it is an opportunity to test the role and extent of any information management systems.

Decisions during the design phase have political as well as practical implications. The framing of the evaluation questions will include some angles and exclude others. The decisions about methodology, the choice of stakeholders as respondents, types of data collection methods and development of tools may privilege some information and some informants over others.

The design stage is an important one from which successes and weaknesses will then hang.

Endnotes

1. Shulman, J. and Asimov, I. (Eds.) (1988) *Isaac Asimov's Book of Science and Nature Quotations*, New York Weidenfeld and Nicolson, cited in O'Leary, Z. (2004) *The Essential Guide to doing Research*, London, Sage, p. 87

8: Methods for Data Collection and its Management

Introduction

This is not a research methods text so there is not going to be extensive discussion of various nuances of social science research. Rather, this chapter explores some broader issues in developing credible and utilisable data sets and is structured in the following way:

1. Approaches and issues in data collection before starting.
2. Bias and triangulation.
3. Working with trusted methods: interview, survey, observation and document analysis.
4. Creative methods for data collection.

Approaches and issues in data collection before starting

Impose some parameters

The right data has to be collected, it has to address the research questions and it has to be in a form and volume which can be analysed. There is no point in collecting data for data's sake, nor amassing so much data that it is impossible to know what to do with it. It is important to determine in advance what is the right cut off point in data collection and to stop then. This will depend on the type of data which is being collected, be it qualitative or quantitative, and the sampling procedures that have been adopted. It is important to keep a clear eye on the types of stakeholders who are responding in case there is a need for booster samples to be added.

There is no point in using data collection methods that alienate prospective respondents because they are long, tedious or simply incomprehensible.

Talk to people and pilot

Talk with people from the stakeholder groups to see how they describe the issues for the evaluation. Do they have a particular language? Are there issues which you may not have thought of which are important to them? Open and exploratory interviewing can help develop research tools which are more meaningful.

Pilot tools and questions with a small number from the target groups, preferably not those who have helped with the scoping exercise above. Fresh eyes are more useful. There are a couple of avenues to explore are this stage:

Understanding

- do they understand what are they being asked to do and why?
- do they understand the purpose of the research, how the data will be used, their role and how long the exercise will take?
- do they have any concerns about the tool itself, how to complete it, the sorts of things they are being asked to do or about confidentiality?

Contributing

- what do their responses contribute to understanding the research questions?
- is the material which they are providing giving insights?

- are their responses addressing the research questions?
- are they offering ideas for developing the intervention (if that is what is being evaluated and that is a component of the evaluation) or taking it forward?
- are there opportunities for any issues to be explored? Is there a clear sense of their role in the intervention?
- is there a clear sense of any benefits and disbenefits which are personally occurring to them?

Taking the time to work through the research questions, and the language and mechanics of the data collection, with members of the target group will do much to improve the quality of the data collected and the experiences both of those responding and those collecting and analysing the data.

Bias and triangulation

Framing and mental models: researcher bias

Everyone has a number of pre-programmed ways of perceiving the world and people. It is a shorthand which stops us having to think thoroughly about everything, but means working with expectations and prejudices. The nature of the frames and mental models[1] which people hold will affect the ways in which respondents answer questions and the ways they may respond to the researcher.

Mental models and frames affect the researcher, what they may take into a situation and the ways in which they may shape an interaction. Trying to access this type of embedded thinking is important.

The world will be shaped for us through our experiences. These will be created and driven by our embodied selves and the ways in which people react to us, for example, through race, gender, physical mobility and age.

On top of this are other types of bias. For example, people experience the world in different ways as sensory, auditory and visual learners. These predispositions affect how a person functions when they are collecting data. Two people, an auditory and a kinaesthetic learner, making an observation of the same event will collect different data. People who are left and right handed will perceive the world differently, the left-hander seeing the world in component parts as opposed to a whole scene; working more with images than language.

Finally there are other sorts of prejudices and predispositions we may hold, and that can mean looking for certain types of things when collecting or analysing the data.

There is no type of data collection or analytic method free of researcher bias when researching social life or indeed within the natural sciences.[2] There is an obligation on anyone entering the field to try to understand what may shape their world-view and bias them. Keeping the Evaluation Log with entries about expectations, feelings which are stirred up during the fieldwork, things which surprised or overturned expectations are all ways to try to explore these types of bias and predisposition.

Triangulation

This is important as a practice in social science research. It gives credibility and reliability to the data which is collected and so confidence to the evaluator that a robust report can be produced.

Triangulation enables the verification or cross-checking of data by collecting data across several sources and using several methods. It is a way of looking at the research questions from several standpoints and so does the best that can be done to overcome the inevitable biases or gaps of a single standpoint or method. Using multiple methods and multiple researchers also helps overcome bias. Denzin (1978)[3] identified four types of triangulation, those of data, investigator, theory and methodology.

A matrix can be developed to show the areas and issues which have been researched and the mode of data collection. This can be included in a final report as an appendix to show the variety of approaches taken to saturate the various issues of the evaluation. For the evaluation team's purposes the matrix can include who undertook particular elements of the research to explore if there are any discernible patterns which may show a bias.

The next section explores methods of data collection. These can support each other. It is imperative to consider respondents, how comfortable they would be with any method and to think about what methods take the evaluation closer to answering the research questions.

Interviews

Interviews are not simply a matter of question and answer. As with all modes of data collection interviews need to be carefully thought through.

There are many ways in which interviews can go wrong. From failing to establish a good interaction, through asking the wrong or a confusing question, and failing to properly record answers. Testing question schedules before using them with the stakeholders who are to be interviewed is important. It is worthwhile thinking through a range of other matters beforehand:

What is the right style of interview? A survey style interview has many closed or limited choice questions. A semi-structured interview has some room for the interviewer to probe answers to open questions. An unstructured interview is run with a topic guide as opposed to questions. The choice will depend on the competence of the researcher, the topics to be explored, the interviewees and the situation in which interviews are taking place, for example, privacy, length of time and the possibilities of using a tape recorder.

What questions get the evaluator closer to understanding the research issues? It is important to test each proposed question against: what does this tell me about the topic? It is important to think carefully about the language in the questions, any assumptions being made, for example that the interviewee knows all about an issue, that an activity was good or a project is bad. These assumptions will create leading questions and so are not helpful. In writing the schedule possible answers can be anticipated but this is no substitute for piloting a schedule. Consider if there is the scope in the interview; think about prompts for more information or follow up questions. It is imperative that questions are not ambiguous.

What language does this group of stakeholders use to talk about the issues? What terminology would each group recognise and respond to best? Trying to couch questions in language and terms which are more readily accessible will help people to warm to the task of answering, make the interviewer feel less intrusive and the interviewee more comfortable.

What question areas may be off-putting? These may be personal questions. They may be ones that put people on the spot making them feel they are being critical or disloyal. They may be questions asking about past failures or mistakes.

How much personal data really needs to be collected? Can broad demographics be used, gender and age for example, in any analysis which include demographic information? Is any demographic data needed and why? It is often a rule of thumb to place more personal questions at the close of a schedule after the other questions have been answered so as not to make people feel put on the spot at the outset. Data Protection Act 1998 needs to be adhered to if personal and identifying data is collected see http://www.ico.gov.uk/for_organisations/data_protection.aspx

What is it about the interviewer which may put off various stakeholders? Think about self-presentation, manner, the ways the research may be presented and any personal elements which may be modified. If there is a team it may be possible to explore allocating interviewers to different groups. It is important to note what effects gender, age and ethnicity may have. The interviewer should note any feelings they have in running an interview, these feelings will be a source of data and say something about the interviewee and the interaction.

What is it about the interviewer which stakeholders may warm to? It is important to establish rapport, to show interest in what is being said, to be authentic and value what is being said and not to be seen to be just exploiting interviewees for the data they can yield.

What might be offered back to interviewees to make them feel more comfortable or valued? This might be assurance about confidentiality, more explanations on how the data will be used, an update on the evaluation as it progresses through e-mail or web-links; it might be the transcript of their interview, if funds allow. It is important to think of ways to offer something back as well as offering your thanks.

How will the answers be recorded? This may be on an interview form if responses are closed, ranking or multiple choice questions. Notes may be taken or tapes made if the interviews are semi structured or unstructured.

Complex speech events

Interviews are more than question and answer. They are marvellous opportunities for misinterpretations. The situation is artificial and the respondents do not know the interviewers in many cases. Even when it is an internal evaluation, they will not know the evaluator in that role. There are many opportunities for misinterpretation, for example, assumptions about having a shared language or frame of reference.

Communication relies on the formulation of a message, sending a message, it travelling across an air space with any number of interferences, being received and decoded. It will be interpreted, there will be the formulation of an answer, sending the answer back again across air space with any amount of interference, for it to be received, decoded and the answer recorded. This is just the easy stuff. Inside the heads of the interviewer and the respondent there will be any amount of interior interferences; thoughts about what to get for dinner, whether last night's episode of Jumping Jack Flash was as good as the previous week's and why Nancy was so short on the telephone this morning. The human capacity for mind wandering needs to be taken into account. Questions need to be clear and answers need to be checked. The whole interview episode needs to be bounded and the respondent needs to know when they are getting close to the end.

Working with colleagues on internal evaluations

This is another glorious opportunity for problems. A schedule needs to be created which reflects the need for the data to address the evaluation research questions. Here it is really important that there are no assumptions made in terms of the language used and no attempts at conceptual shorthand. It is hard for colleagues to interview colleagues; they can be concerned about coming across as silly, as difficult, or as not knowing something which they should. It is however more important to be thorough and to ask for explanations than to make assumptions. In these situations, expectations, shared organisational or professional cultures and frames will be out in force to trip up the data collection process.

The best ways to deal with concerns are prefacing the interviewing by acknowledging that some of the questions might sound pedestrian but that it is important for the interviewer not to make assumptions just because they know something of the organisation or the programme. The interviewer will need to self-check to make sure that they are asking for clarification as the interview proceeds. 'I know what I think I understand by . . . but could you tell me what . . . means to you?' may be helpful sorts of questions to have in mind as the evaluation interview proceeds.

There is a risk of the respondent playing an issue up or down depending what they think the interviewer representing the evaluation might want to hear. Again the interviewer needs to be careful to check out what is meant and to ask for examples.

Interviewing superordinates

This too is hard. The evaluator needs to go into their research role and try only to focus on the task to be done. The usual rules of rapport building, the importance of explaining the research and confidentiality need to be adhered to. The pace of the interview needs to match the respondent but there it has to be borne in mind that the interview should not be rushed through some internal sense of the need to get out of the superior's office or to not take up more time.

It is important to not make assumptions and as with colleagues to question understandings.

Again, if the researcher has strong feelings or expectations before the interview it is worth recording these as data, as it is to note any strong reactions when running the interview.

Interviewing beneficiaries

If this is an internal evaluation and the beneficiary is in the evaluator's organisation then the importance of emphasising confidentiality cannot be overdone. The interviewee may be overly concerned about complaining or with trying to be positive about their experiences. The questions need to be carefully constructed so there is a high level of internal validity to check for such tendencies.

It is important that beneficiaries do not feel coerced into having to be involved in interviews. There may be other formats that would work better for them.

Working with translators and interpreters

There are issues to be thought through in working with translators and interpreters. Not least of all allowing extra time for the interview and ensuring that the person doing the work is a reliable translator or interpreter. It is sometimes harder to establish rapport when working through another person. It is important to keep open body language, to maintain interest and eye contact with the interviewee and to also extend the same interest to the interpreter or translator. It is worth bearing in mind that there will be less scope for off the cuff comments and exploring additional lines of enquiry than may usually be the case with semi and unstructured interviews.

Before working on the interview with a translator or interpreter it is important to brief them about the interview, the ground that it will cover and to check that they understand and have a chance to ask questions. They will after all be presenting your project to the interviewee and it is important that they do not have any misconceptions or uncertainties otherwise there are further risks of injecting inaccuracies into the interview.

After the interview

It is important to write up after each interview impressions from the interview, to re-read notes taken and to flesh them out. Memory can be fallible and interviews can get blurred. If notes were taken in an interview these should be written up more fully. Any in-interview interpretations and associations should be revisited and fleshed out in the context of the now completed interview.

Surveys

Creating a survey is often the first thing which springs to mind when people think about collecting data. There are many very poor quality surveys out there to show for it. Many are written up as reports with great authority but really say nothing at all. There are no short cuts in writing surveys. They need a huge amount of patience in drafting and re-drafting. There are no opportunities to be beside the respondent to check that they understand the questions:

- does this question give me the answer that I need to better understand the research question?
- does the respondent understand this question?
- is there any ambiguity?
- does this answer format give me the information that I need to work with the data?

Surveys for evaluations are likely to be descriptive surveys which are finding out something of the demographics of respondents, something about their use of a service or programme, and what their attitudes are to a service, programme or issue.

There may be surveys which ask the same questions, of the same group over time in order to track any changes in attitudes and behaviours as a result of the survey.

Assuming the survey is on-line or paper then it needs to be framed with information about its intended use, its importance for the research, how it is to be completed and returned. It needs to include a thank you for doing the survey and inform the respondent how to get more information about the project. A survey can be administered orally if there are issues with respondents' possible literacy or capacity to complete the form.

Surveys traditionally use questions which have pre-coded answers as below:

I. Lickert scales
All people coming into the hostel should go to a relapse prevention programme as part of the condition of entry. 1=strongly disagree 5=strongly agree

Strongly disagree	Disagree	Unsure	Agree	Strongly agree
1	2	3	4	5

2. Complete the blank
How frequently do you use the needle exchange in any month? _____ times

This is a difficult question on two grounds:

- people may feel that there is a socially acceptable answer and try to guess what that would be. This is especially so if the question is asked of them
- it requires people to think back and recollect. Memories can be false and it may be a painful issue. In this question there really is no specified timeframe in which they are to reflect, they are asked to do an averaging exercise about their use

Possibly ask about the last complete month and a supplementary question as to whether this was more or less than other months.

3. Yes/No
If there was a mobile needle exchange in Letchworth would you use it?

Yes _____

No _____

Don't know _____

Always have a 'don't know' box for all survey questions. Don't know is not the same as neutral and it is an answer that has to be provided for.

4. Ranking

Please list these five suggestions for using your evening time in your order of preference

More counselling	Education classes	Relapse prevention classes	More outdoor work and gym	More NA groups

This assumes that respondents have the concentration to work through the list and that there are no ties between responses they want to make.

5. Selecting from a list

Underline the topic for the new class which you prefer best

Art classes	Photography classes	Computer classes	Gym	Horticulture

This assumes respondents will like one and that there are no first equals. Also think about the language is there anything wrong with 'you would like best'. Do people know what horticulture is? Have people the same ideas about what the other classes might be?

Surveys have to be piloted. Ideally sit with people after they have gone through the schedule to see what they thought of it, question by question.

Observation

There is much written about observation techniques and the ways in which observation may be approached as a participant or as a simple observer. There are issues here about covert and overt observation which are important ethical issues, see Chapter 4. For an evaluation the observations should only be overt. But while moving around a project site for example, observations will be made and inevitably inferences drawn. This however is not admissible unless revisited as a formal observation. It might spark questions, for example if the numbers of people in an activities session was overly low, and you may question why this was so, or if there were long queues for food and why this might have been so.

The Evaluation Log is a good place to store random observations and to see if it helps develop new lines of enquiry or triangulates with other data. These observations need to be checked.

Formal observations will need to be undertaken according to a schedule devised for the data being sought, otherwise attention can drift to other details. If there is a team of observers people will be attracted to different things and even two people observing the same situation will see different scenes if there is not a guide schedule. People see and filter material according to the ways in which they see the world or their preoccupations in the world.

The schedule should reflect the need for certain types of data that address the research questions. The schedule should be trialled to make sure it is comprehensible and that it solicits the right data with multiple observers.

Before starting on observations be rigorous and note down any expectations or preconceptions. It is better to try to surface and acknowledge internal blinders. If these elements then appear in the observation notes (double check yourself) were they sought or were they really there and as dominant or otherwise as your records show them to be?

Check your notes and expectations with others as a source of external policing.

There are various ways of seeking observation data. Examples could include:

- focus on one or two participants in an activity session for the whole activity period noting everything they are doing and all their interactions over 10 minute intervals
- focus on issues such as health and safety, tuition styles
- focus on group dynamics and how these are managed, who dominates and who is excluded

Observation schedules can range from the structured, through semi-structured (allowing for the capture of unsought data) on to the completely unstructured where the observer seeks to capture the look and feel of something.

Stay with the observation for the pre-determined time. For example, the length of an activity session, but in determining the length of time, think about including the start-up and the wind-down of the activity where there may be interesting material to note.

Observations can be checked through with other observers of the same event or with another involved in the event. Caution needs to be taken with the latter course of action. It is wise to check out what may have been misunderstood, or have seemed exceptional and to check a couple of facts to explore understandings and impressions before writing up the observation notes. Ways into checking could include asking the person leading the activity how they thought it went, what they thought worked well, what else they might have liked to have been included. These open and general questions will generate a sense of a broader context for what has been observed.

Observations need to be repeated to see if there are patterns or the observation was a one off. Observation notes need to record patterns in the observed data, your own responses to the observed data and how this may have affected what was observed and to note any difficulties or issues which were raised which warrant re-checking. Notes should be written according to the observer schedule which itself should address the research issues.

The write ups will ultimately be analysed for what they have captured in relation to the research issues and for any unintended issues they may have raised.

Observations may be used both within overall paradigm of positivist or experimental research or a part of a constructive approach.

Document analysis

This is working with pre-prepared documents and other media. These might be:

- *literature reviews and web searching.* This broad contextual material may put the programme or organisation being evaluated in a context. It may generate some ideas for the recommendations section about alternative approaches or ways of viewing problems, it may give some sense that the issues the programme or organisation is tackling are presenting difficulties to other organisations, it may help create some sense of how well the organisation is doing. This is not comparative research it is context setting. This needs to be stressed
- *statistics and reports*, for example Local Council documents, HM Government Inspection Reports, surveys and reports from pressure or lobby groups, may also help create context about the work being evaluated, it may show gaps in provision, or other approaches to the issue
- *monitoring* and other data already collected by the programme or organisation being evaluated

- *desk review* of materials produced by and about the organisation, its work, ethos, philosophy of the programme or interventions, policies, information on staffing and reports in the press

Materials may be of many types: personal and official communications, letters, memos, e-mails or journals; they may cover finances, they may be from various media, journals, papers, documentaries; they may be contemporary or historical; they may be reports, summaries and presentations of statistics or prose.

The data needs to be interrogated in a systematic way otherwise it would be easy to drown in the material. Before starting it is important to have a clear idea of the types of data which are to be collected from the documents. Think about this as like creating an interview schedule, but for the documents. This is not to exclude the unexpected or interesting, but bring to the exercise a sense of purpose and direction in order to answer the research questions.

Firstly **review** the material item by item:

- what does the material say about the issue being evaluated, the organisation?
- does it help or should it be discarded?

This will give an overview of what is really helpful and what is not. It will provide some orientation to the pile of resources and what approaches to take. Reviewing may show up contradictions or repetitions. For example, several documents may repeat the same fact or statement and so seem to establish a weight of evidence. In reviewing the documents it is worth noting whether this is based on one resource or multiple sources. Recombining the same evidence does not mean it is weighty evidence, it is just repetition.

Keep some preliminary notes of any of these types of observations.

If documents are retained then **explore** them systematically.

Establish its genesis, authenticity and credibility as a text:

- who wrote it?
- for what office?
- for what purpose?
- what's the agenda?
- what is verifiable in the document?
- is there any obvious bias?
- does one document or other source back another?
- does the documentary material serve to triangulate other data gathered for example from interviews?

Interrogate the material having established the above.

The document is reviewed for occurrences of the data which are being looked for. Note the frequencies of the mentions of the sought data, the volume of the mention and anything about the context which sheds light on the issue mentioned.

Undertake an interrogation of the material, as you would interview a respondent. Assume the document can provide answers to questions that take you to a more advanced understanding of the research questions. Highlight the passages in the document which answer each of the questions on your pre-prepared schedule. Keep notes of unexpected but relevant material and on omissions that you may not have expected to find.

Creative methods for data collection

The following are some ways in which data might be collected from different groups who may feel less comfortable in formal interview situations or working through a survey.

However the idea of working more creatively to unlock perceptions should not be limited to service users: staff, trustees and other stakeholders should also be offered alternative modes of exploration and expression. These methods may reveal more essential or more unexpected points.

Role plays are one way to get a small group of people to explore their service needs or any issues with the topic being evaluated. It is a way for service users to perhaps explore what their perceptions are of the ways in which the service they receive is delivered. It is a powerful method and can offer some stunning insights which may not otherwise have been accessed. It is a way to explore 'out of the box ideas' by getting people to think about what would work for them.

Likewise staff and other stakeholders can explore elements of service delivery and their organisation through role plays, perhaps thinking about the service in five years time if it goes on as it is or what it might be like at its best.

This requires great trust and promised confidentiality. It is a powerful way to surface concerns and hopes. These exercises can set markers much in the way of taking a solution focus to working on issues of service delivery over the medium term.

Photographs can be taken by different groups of stakeholders to show what is important to them, significantly good or bad about their organisation or programme and so on. The photos and explanations can be shared with a group to prompt some focused discussion.

Draw and write is a way to work with people who may not want to, or cannot, write much. Exploring the answers can be done one to one or in a small group setting if that is not intimidating. In response to questions people can either draw or write or a combination of both. A researcher or observer will need to take notes of what they say to go alongside their own responses.

Continua is where people are asked to range themselves along an imaginary line drawn on the floor. Either end of the line represents an extreme point, for example extremely good or very bad, relating to the evaluation topic. Ask people to place themselves on the line at the point which marks their opinion. This is shared with the group.

Sculpting response to questions. People work on their own or in pairs to produce a tableau or pose. Go around the group and capture all tableau with a camera and record a quick explanation of it. A group review can then follow with people re-striking their tableau and exploring the explanations in more depth.

Photo diaries can be produced to capture people's thoughts about what is of significance to them about the evaluation topic. They can choose to capture significant in-programme events or issues and to find things from their broader lives which may be important to them. There may be interactions between for example, the intervention and their broader lives which they are able to synthesise in these ways.

Audio and video diaries can also be used to enable participants to record what they want to say about the evaluation topic. They may have their own recorders on their mobiles or may go to a designated space to record their thoughts, feelings and opinions. These can be used as and when people want or there can be allocated times for making the recordings. The data of course will vary depending on a regular making of the diary or being prompted by an event.

Reflective diaries can be kept by participants in which they reflect on their experiences, their learning, difficulties and frustrations and what may be working for them.

These can have a few structured questions or, after a briefing, be left as open spaces for people to respond to as they wish – writing, drawings, cuttings, collages or whatever they want to include can be included. They are to be a learning experience and sense making experience as well as a record.

Blogs work as diaries. The access to them needs to be considered.

Mapping an intervention that is seeking to impact the community in some way can be achieved by asking people to walk around their community and map it. For example in terms of the issues which are important to them, important places in terms of the ways in which the community has improved or where there may be unmet need. This graphic representation and supporting narrative may do much to enable discussion of where there is impact, where and why there may be gaps and unmet need.

Timelines are personal maps. Ask for a lifeline to be drawn with the peaks and troughs of life drawn in. There should be a timeframe and a theme set to encourage participants to explore their perceptions of the issue being evaluated or place it in the context of broader life events and needs. This would give insight through discussions into the efficacy of what is being evaluated or the types of personal and social contexts it is operating in. It may highlight new developmental areas for future work or the cultivation of organisational and operational partnerships.

These methods require people to be able to talk about their experiences in public, not be intimidated and not feel any need to follow others. There is a need to manage these activities within the envelope of confidentiality and to make people feel safe.

Graffiti walls can be created on large sheets of paper by asking people to offer their ideas and opinions. These can be in response to a specific question or can be left blank.

Evaluation wheel Draw a circle and divide it into segments according to the areas on which judgment is sought. For example the elements that went into a residential programme: accommodation, activities and food. Ask people to tick the top three things they liked. Ask people to initial their ticks or issue people with different colours to prevent multiple voting.

Sticky dots is another system for voting. Generate a list of ideas within the group, for example, things they found most useful, or concerns they want to see addressed. Write these on flip chart paper. Issue people with a finite number of different coloured dots and ask them to use them to vote.

Post it notes will allow participants to give feedback on an activity which has just been run. Ask for a word or phrase which best describes how people feel on the post-it note and ask people to stick these to sheets of A1 paper on the wall.

Card sorts Playing-card sized cards are pre-printed with statements with some left blank. People are asked in pairs to sort the cards into categories. These should be categories that are about strong likes, dislikes and concerns. Categories might include the following: Things we find most useful about the programme; Things we hate; Things we want more of; Things we find motivational; Things that have to be improved. Having sorted cards into the piles and added any of their own statements, the pairs might be asked to rank the cards or reduce them to their top three. The cards might cover statements about a programme, an organisation, working conditions, personal aspirations, community needs and so on. The idea is to capture responses and the underlying discussion.

These ideas can be captured as a group and some ideas might be moved into an action plan.

Summing up

This chapter has offered an overview of a number of ways of thinking about data collection. It has stressed the importance of thinking about data collection in relation to research questions, stakeholders, practicalities like time, place and researcher competence. It has offered some more innovative ways to collect data from a range of stakeholders.

Endnotes

1. See Chapter 4, Squirrell, G. (2011) *Engagement in Action.* Lyme Regis, Russell House Publishing. Frames are ways in which the world can be constructed for us, for example through the media, and so we respond to situations and events with a set of pre-defined and media created lenses. Mental models are the ways in which our life experiences and significant others have affected how we see the world. For example, if we have had many experiences of rejection or failing in social situations we will interpret social events as threatening and as likely to end in this kind of disaster for us. Inevitably it will.
2. Scientists are social actors as well as scientists and will take into their labs their roles in broader social life along with their expertise. This will influence their research and their attitudes towards it.
3. Denzin, N.K. (1978) *The Research Act.* 2nd edn. New York, McGraw Hill.

9: Participatory Evaluation

Introduction

Participatory evaluation has a very clear democratic political basis. It is learning for action and for change. It is a very specific methodology which some may view as risky. It is and should be without the controls and checks that may protect certain stakeholders' interests over others, which may be found in some more traditional forms of commissioned evaluation. It is a co-created and co-owned form of evaluation.

Participation may be undertaken through a range of roles and to different degrees, but even where the amount of participation may be less, there still remains accountability to a broader stakeholder group. It is a very definite and different approach to evaluation.

Much work on participatory monitoring and evaluation has been informed by international development work. This chapter explores participatory evaluation as it is developing with programmes in the UK, Europe and the US. It looks at participatory evaluation in relation to work with young people. It outlines the integration of participatory evaluation into community-based dialogues which are part of community development work. Much of this dialogue-based work continues to be in international development work.

The chapter is in six sections:

- defining features of participatory evaluation
- the elements of participatory evaluation
- benefits and possible pitfalls in participatory evaluation
- some methods of participatory evaluation
- undertaking participatory evaluation with young people
- extending participatory monitoring and evaluation into communities' dialogues and development

Defining features of participatory evaluation

The Institute of Development Studies at the University of Sussex (1998)[1] defined participatory evaluation as:

> . . . not just a matter of using participatory techniques within a conventional monitoring and evaluation setting. It is about radically re-thinking who initiates and undertakes the process, and who learns or benefits from the findings.

Power and extended participation

This is the heart of participatory evaluation, the conscious redistribution of power and of the understanding of knowledge, its generation and use. It differs from more conventional evaluations in that it seeks to co-engage a broad range of stakeholders in the framing of the evaluation, in fashioning its questions, its operation and use of the data. It is an evaluation out in the open: its purpose, intentions for use and the ways in which it may be used for change are tabled clearly from the outset. There is an expectation for delivery against a collectively fashioned agenda and co-accountability across all the stakeholder groups that this will be so.

Central to many instances of participatory evaluation are the perspectives, concerns, interests, preferences, and decisions of those who are often the least powerful in society. Those who are often the most done-to and most affected as stakeholders. The evaluation is generated, designed and undertaken from the multiple socio-economic, cultural and political contexts of all participating stakeholders. This way of working requires time and sensitivity on everyone's part in order to best develop a common language, common understanding and connectedness.

Learning and change
Participatory evaluation is undertaken for the learning that can be derived from it and it is geared towards improvement and development. There are no experts: everyone can contribute their perspectives to generating learning and thinking about the ways in which changes can be developed and what those changes might be. Participatory evaluations are future-oriented, looking for solutions through taking actions. They are less likely to look for blame than some traditional evaluations, learning from where things work well as well as where things did not work.[2]

Support for participatory evaluation
In participatory evaluations the expert evaluators have a supportive role, they are experts in their field, but their role is about teaching others as well as using their technical expertise. Participatory evaluation costs are heavy in terms of time and resources. For example if a programme is being evaluated then the staff will need release time to be involved in discussions and decision-making about the evaluation, and they will need to be trained and to have time to undertake data collection and analysis. There will need to be expert support for all stakeholders. The training may involve on-going support and coaching as the evaluation proceeds, particularly in the process of data analysis and in developing conclusions and making decisions.

The fact that the decision for this type of evaluation comes from within a community or organisation and that it is concerned very much with learning and improving can mean that funding for the evaluation is harder to raise than for a conventional expert led evaluation. More conventional evaluations may have more focus on communicable outputs for a donor, the development of generalisable knowledge and some contribution to the body of academic or research-based knowledge. This broader application may make them more attractive to fund.

Given potential concerns about the time involved, the need for expert support, the need to raise funding and possibly less credibility being accorded to the outputs from participatory evaluation, there have to be high levels of commitment to undertake this type of evaluation.

It is not possible to bail out part way through and leave it to an expert. That is to leave a community with a sense of failing.

Approaches
Participatory evaluations may make use of traditional data collection methods but they are really distinguished by the emphasis on group work and on more reflective and creative methods. Participatory evaluation relies on methods derived from Participatory Rapid Appraisal (PRA). These methods are intended to be more engaging for marginalised groups. They are intended to promote discussions, problem identification, analysis, problem solving and formulating corrective actions.

The elements of participatory evaluation
This section explores some of the particular elements of the participatory evaluation process and the roles that may be played by expert evaluators and members of communities.

An overview of the participatory evaluation process
The process has been described as a 'spiral of key learning moments'.[3] This seems fitting because it captures a number of elements, the importance of the conscious and reflective learning at all stages,

which as the chapter will demonstrate is central to the participatory evaluation structure. The spiral captures the dynamic, evolving and exciting quality of the evaluation as something moving upwards because of, and as part of, its process.

Roles for stakeholders

There are a number of ways in which stakeholders may want to be involved in participatory evaluations. Some may want full participation from the outset, involved in all stages of discussions, training activities, collecting and working with the data and exploring potential change actions. Others may prefer more partial roles. Some may prefer to hang back a little at the outset and do more as they become more confident and familiar with the process. Participatory evaluations should be flexible enough to accommodate the development of stakeholders' interests and capacity.

Partial roles may include:

- acting as consultants to the experts to help inform them of the issues from their experiences which are the subject of the evaluation and help to provide context
- acting as discussants in the planning process and at subsequent phases, for example, helping to identify other groups of stakeholders, exploring the implications of the findings
- helping with elements of the work, for example data collection

Roles for experts

It is essential that the expert evaluators play several and clear roles throughout participatory evaluation. The experts need to have a number of skills to enable them to undertake these roles.

They need to:

- be able communicators with a range of different stakeholders
- have effective evaluation skills
- be willing to share their skills
- be willing to teach others
- be willing to support the development of others
- be able to coach and support the participant-evaluators at various stages of the work
- know when to move to the sidelines and when to return to provide more hands on help
- be able to work as colleagues with the participant-evaluators as needed

Using this range of skills and their sensitivities the experts need to be able to do the following:

- they need to teach the knowledge that they have of evaluation process, design and execution
- they need to help the participant-evaluators to link their developing new knowledge of evaluation with their own tacit knowledge
- they need to be skilled as facilitators to draw out from participants their local and specialist knowledge of the context and of the topic being evaluated. This will ensure that the right research questions are formulated, ones in which there is real interest, have real meaning and be ones that will help to focus future action
- they need to have group management skills and be sensitive to group dynamics in order that all within the groups of participant-evaluators feel able to speak and that they are not at risk within the group of being betrayed or dominated
- they need to be able to help meet the participant-evaluators' training needs in understanding the evaluation purpose and the processes involved, in planning, in devising the right field tools and deploying them, in data analysis and in developing evaluation outputs to inform subsequent phases of decision-making

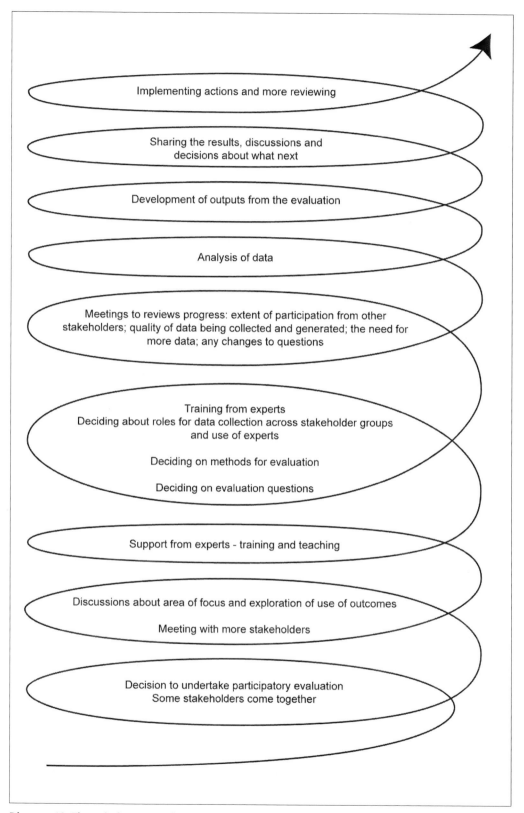

Diagram 19: The spiral process of participatory evaluations

- they may need to be involved in some data collection but should be able to work in co-worker as opposed to specialist roles in order that the participant-evaluators' skills and confidence can build
- they need to be able to skilfully move from perhaps playing more central roles to the periphery of the group. Helping hold and contain the group's concerns and anxieties as it moves through progressive phases of designing tools, undertaking data collection and returning to begin review and data analysis
- they need to be able to identify when there may be problems ahead and suggest meetings, or call in additional support
- they need to be able to learn alongside the participant-evaluators
- they need to be able to engage in honest reflection about their own roles and those of the participant-evaluators and share these reflections

Designing and implementing the participatory evaluation

There will be, as with any evaluation, a number of early decisions to be taken. The experts and the stakeholders need to move through the following stages. These may be iterative discussions until the stakeholders feel comfortable to move on:

1. Deciding on purpose. The main purpose will be for learning for improvement in the identified area. Deciding on the various objectives of the evaluation.
2. Deciding whether participatory evaluation is the right methodology.
3. Deciding with stakeholders who are to be involved in the evaluation and in which capacities. For example as members of the core team taking the evaluation work forward, as members of a steering or reference group, or as contributors of data.
4. The stakeholders should determine the questions to explore and then develop specific questions.
5. Decisions need to be taken about how data might be collected to address these questions. The stakeholders need to determine the best method for the data to be collected, which stakeholders or community members should be involved, how they might be approached and any ethical issues inherent in the data collection.
6. The stakeholders need to decide how they want to talk about the participatory evaluation, its purpose, questions, methods, ethics and aspirations to those they wish to approach or they wish would support them.
7. There may be training to be undertaken to manage the various methods.
8. There will need to be the development of a timetable and means of checking that all the necessary tasks have been done.
9. Data collection.
10. Reporting back on progress, learning how to identify emergent issues.
11. More data collection, making sure that there is some triangulation of the data. This may be particularly important if there are some dominant community voices which wish to impose their perspectives through the data collection process.
12. Detailed analysis and development of ways to report.
13. Discussions of findings and agreeing on actions.

There is nothing overly unusual about these stages. The stakeholders will be supported by experts who will provide training and coaching and will also take on co-worker roles.

Planning the practicalities of the work

Given that so much of the work involved in the participatory evaluation will be new to the stakeholders, and it is important that everyone understands the range of tasks, the links between tasks, resources needed and how to manage time, it is suggested that a method such as the Gantt Charting process outlined below is used. This has value for several reasons. It is a great teaching tool, it externalises and makes clear the processes and resource needs. It is important that the stakeholders understand what is involved, and their commitments. The Gantt Chart process, or something similar, may be useful in teaching transferable and organisational skills. Most importantly it is imperative to tie these basic elements of the project down or there will be frustration and the project could fall apart and it is important that there is success.

The following are helpful steps.

1. List the tasks which need to be done.
2. Rather than assuming a task is what it may seem to be at face value, encourage the stakeholders to break the task into its component parts. For example, while running a focus group may only take a half-day, there are associated tasks which need to be undertaken and the whole activity will require a lot more than a half-day. These task parts include:
   - training those to run the focus group, including their having been involved as participants in other groups
   - determining the topic for the focus group
   - determining the range of stakeholders to be invited to explore the topic
   - sorting a venue and time, bearing in mind the range of possible commitments and needs of the stakeholders for example crèche facilities and refreshments
   - inviting representatives of various stakeholder groups and some back-ups
   - buying refreshments
   - readying the venue
   - running the focus groups
   - thanking participants
   - debriefing
   - clearing the venue
   - working up the notes from the focus group
   - analysing the data
   - sharing data with colleagues

This puts a different complexion on running the focus group. Now there is a need for perhaps a small team rather than just a facilitator and note taker. Maybe there is a need to run more than one focus group to better explore the issue and maybe this helps given that there is a need to send out a number of invitations to ensure that the range of people needed and who are invited do attend.

Clearly there are a number of tasks to undertake in setting up the focus group, some of which are dependent on others. There are a number of different time demands for these tasks. Working through each element in this way will help ensure an accurate understanding of the activities and the commitments.

3. Discussions will need to focus on working through all the tasks, any dependencies between task elements, the key milestones which the stakeholders want to meet, the time budget for each task once all its steps are understood and who is to take responsibility. The charting is an active, external activity with an end product that is a visual representation all can share. The Gantt Chart can be easily reproduced. Learning and thinking about planning in this way is also a useful transferable skill, a point to be made. List all of these tasks and milestones.

Projects fall apart because task dependencies are not appreciated, the time needed to complete a task is not properly budgeted for and people do not work within the essential time windows. Working through the Gantt process is a way to reduce the risk of some of these issues.

4. Undertake the Gantt Charting process. Brainstorm a list of all tasks. List these tasks in column 1. Note dependencies between elements in column 2. Explore time required according to the following formula. Allocate to each task three possible time estimates: worst, most likely and absolute best. Then derive estimated time using the formula $(B + 4 \times ML + W) \div 6$.

Task List	Dependencies	Worst time (W)	Most Likely (ML)	Best Time (B)	Calculated Estimate
A	None				
B	A before B				
C	None				
D	A and B				

Use the information about dependencies and the calculated estimated time to complete a Gantt Chart (Diagram 20).

5. The Gantt Chart can be reviewed and if necessary tweaked as the evaluation team meets. It will be important to think about contingency plans if there is serious slippage in getting tasks completed, as there is a move towards a milestone or if a fresh task cannot be started because something has not been finished.

6. Review progress against the Gantt Chart. These sessions need to be run on the basis of exploring any obstacles, barriers and facilitating factors. It is not helpful to apportion blame. Difficulties in getting started, the need for more training, problems with lack of confidence or know how and acknowledging the task size was underestimated are all important learning points. Learning may be about individuals, shortfalls in training or there may be wider and systemic issues which need to be explored, such as resistances amongst community members. This is all data and will need discussions, reflection and actions. The more difficult issues to resolve may be where systemic blockages are discovered. This will require action.

Benefits and possible pitfalls in participatory evaluation

There are many benefits from participatory evaluation and some possible pitfalls. These are outlined in this section.

The benefits include:

- capacity development of a range of stakeholders in skills related to evaluation and research
- developing literacy in research methods and in reading research and evaluation outputs
- development of a range of transferable skills such as those to do with planning an activity, understanding more about management of time and financial resources
- for some stakeholders, the development of their communication skills and evidence to support such claims

Task No.	Task Name	Task dependencies	Calculated estimated time	People responsible	Week 1	Week 2	Week 3	Week 4	Week 5	Week 6	Week 7	Week 8 etc.

Put lines in the length of task.

Link with vertical lines the task/s which need to be completed before others can begin or be completed, show the links in terms of the task length of line.

Put in milestones as △ – these may be reports and presentations.

If there is a risk assessment and extra time has been budgeted for some tasks then show the bonus time in another colour.

Mark the review dates on the chart for the PME team.

Diagram 20: Gantt Charting

- greater communication between different stakeholder groups and a greater appreciation of others' perspectives
- amongst both stakeholders and organisations, the development of a greater appreciation of the roles which can be played by monitoring and evaluation and the ways in which these can contribute to the development of programmes and to organisational learning
- for some stakeholders experiential learning and opportunities to develop skills which may help in accessing employment, for example working with others, negotiation and discussion, time keeping, taking responsibility for task completion
- developing a rich and grounded understanding of the issue being evaluated
- developing learning informed actions
- having commitment to taking actions forward as there was investment in the earlier stages of the work
- working throughout with agreement and shared understandings
- having effective support from experts willing to share their skills, knowledge and to support the participant evaluators and the process. This reduces risk of damage to any people who are involved
- starting the process of a virtuous cycle of participatory evaluation, development of action goals which can then be evaluated as they are implemented
- development of leadership skills and leaders within stakeholder groups
- stakeholders will have a sense of agency that can offer a of number of other benefits, such as greater self-esteem, health benefits and the development of a sense of future directions and purpose
- any organisations involved in the participatory evaluation should derive organisational learning and may have a more grounded place within their communities of stakeholders
- the expert evaluators should have developed their own skills, personal insights and capacity for this sort of work

The potential pitfalls that may need to be managed can include the following:

- as with any participatory work there are issues of power and holding the balance of power between stakeholders who may be more and less adept at its manipulation. There is a key role for the facilitators, consultants and evaluation professionals to play in ensuring that everyone who needs to be is trained and understands their role and can play their part. They need to make sure in facilitating discussions and supporting decision making about the evaluation purpose, design and use of findings that one set of voices does not dominant. They need to support all participants so there is the development of personal confidence and confidence in the process
- there is a danger in spending too much energy on the processes, on discussion of group dynamics and the learning so that some of the harder and core needs of the evaluation get down-played or lost
- it is important to put time into the planning process and making good use of resources. There can be temptations to skimp on the work of planning at the risk of jeopardising the evaluation outcomes because people are keen to get on with the actual work, as they see it, or because time is limited
- there is a need to invest time in training people to undertake the evaluative work
- there is a need for sensible goal setting and not to try to get in too much data or get it too quickly. People's expectations need to be managed

- there is a danger that more emphasis is placed on the creativity of the participatory techniques and less on the quality of the emerging data
- there is a need for rigour in setting objectives for the evaluation, in data collection and in ensuring that the data is verifiable and can be triangulated
- there have to be effective cycles for review and examination so the highest standards can be met
- there are risks that the outputs of the evaluation will not be taken so seriously as a conventional evaluation by those external to the process, funders or those setting policy for example
- it is a solely subjective way of working which flies in the face of more positivistic designs, which can lead to it being dismissed
- there is a question to ask. This is do people define themselves as marginalised? In need of help and support from experts? Do they want to be treated as such and so involved in community developments and integrating participatory evaluation into their lives?

Some methods of participatory evaluation

Research methods

The methods for participatory evaluation can include a number of those outlined in Chapter 9, for example, interviews may be run with key stakeholders, there may be surveys and there may be observations. These tools will be used in similar ways in traditional and participatory evaluations, all the requirements for effective design and piloting apply. However, there may be less emphasis on getting such large samples, there may be more emphasis on working with oral methods, such as interviews, over written surveys.

The emphasis in participatory evaluation is on the more creative and discursive methods to engage people in the evaluation, especially those who might not naturally want to do this type of work. The emphasis is on learning and on generating solutions and actions and this may require different types of approaches.

In addition other methods, some of which were offered in Chapter 8, may include:

- testimonials
- story telling
- social mapping
- trend analysis
- time lines
- impact drawings
- chuff charts and other visual or kinaesthetic choice and ranking exercises
- diaries
- focus groups

A few of these methods not explored in Chapter 8 are offered below and see http://www.e2rc.net for further participatory research methods. An outline for running focus groups is also offered below.

Methods for working, training and evaluating

It is important to remember that there will be a number of meetings, discussions and training events which develop and support the processes of participatory evaluation. These will need to be well facilitated so stakeholders remain engaged. It is likely that these events will include a number of games and activities which support the development of communication skills, team development and self-awareness. Some activities will need to be energisers and mood changers to keep attention focused within the room as opposed to attention leaking out to external preoccupations.

These activities will need to be evaluated to understand what learning took place and the degree to which people felt that their learning needs had been met. Quick evaluations and check-ins can be used which include:

- evaluation wheels
- reactionnaires
- post-its
- group rounds
- sticky dots
- graffiti walls
- short questions evaluations:
  - ○ three things I can use from today are . . .
  - ○ with hindsight I wish that I had asked about . . .
  - ○ something I am still unsure about is . . .

Again see http://www.e2rc.net for materials for training workshops and evaluation tools.

Some selected participatory methods follow.

Testimonials

This is a loosely structured way to gather some specific accounts from stakeholders.

This involves:

- a stakeholder prepared to talk openly and at some length about an agreed topic
- an evaluation partner who questions. This person is not an interviewer but an evaluation partner with a topic guide to help the raconteur to stay on track
- the wherewithal to tape the session so it can be transcribed

Topic areas which may be of use to explore could include:

- talk about your life before the programme/intervention
- how has involvement with the programme/intervention made a difference to your life
- what hopes or plans do you have for your future, what are you taking from the programme/ intervention to help you

These are big questions which can and will range off into the individual's life, their family, friends, employment, lifestyle, accommodation, their relationship with and perceptions of their community and so on. A topic guide is a set of a few questions which help explore the main area and keep the raconteur on track. The questions might explore value of an intervention, any unmet need, how the programme helped and so on.

Testimonials bring a detailed and rich data to the evaluation. They will highlight issues that may not otherwise have been thought about. They bring very detailed and very personal material and this can be used to help explore and explain more about individual lives, impacts and community experiences.

A testimonial will probably take about 30 minutes to collect. The transcription rather more time. The raconteur should be offered a copy of their testimonial to see if there is anything they want to add, they may want to offer a reflection on their testimonial, having had time to think further after the opportunity to talk.

A collection of testimonials, a photo of the person or something from their testimonial will make a good display, actual or virtual, for others in the community to share their experiences and to talk about in relation to their needs.

Impact drawings

These are personal snap shots of the impact of certain life events.

Ask stakeholders not to worry about the artwork but to use marker pens to try to draw out some quick sketches of for example:

- life before the programme
- involvement on the programme
- hopes for the future

These can be used as starting points for sharing narratives about what it has meant to be involved in the programme being evaluated or topic being evaluated. These narratives should be taped and transcribed so they can run alongside the drawings. These might be used as a display. The material can be used as data, exploring key themes and issues. The artifacts themselves used to illustrate the findings of the evaluation.

This is an open way to explore issues and previously unconsidered issues may emerge. This will give some ideas for the types of futures that people want and ways that these needs might be met.

Programme time line

Again a pen and paper activity which can be undertaken on large sheets of paper. The drawings will spark narrative accounts which can be shared within the group.

The stakeholders are asked to draw a time line. This might be in three sections:

Firstly their lives prior to the programme, some of the significant themes and events in their lives, what brought stakeholders to their involvement in the programme.

Secondly, time on the programme.

Thirdly, an extension to the time line, a projection as to what time post-programme might be like if they are able to carry forward their learning and things which they hope the programme can give them. They can in this section include other elements which may not yet be in existence on the programme but which they would find useful.

The time-lines and the narratives provide personal reflection, insight into individuals' lives and the links between themselves, their communities and the programme. The creative extensions might generate ideas for action.

Community or social mapping

A tool to contextualise where the project operates physically and within people's social realities and understand more about stakeholders' perceptions of the project and community.

Working in groups stakeholders are asked to draw maps including: community structures, institutions, associations, kinship groupings, boundaries and resources. They can add to their maps those elements they would like to see within their communities. These might be elements which the project or programme could provide.

They can mark on their maps any community elements with which they feel they have developed stronger associations as a result of programme involvement.

Focus groups

These are group interviews and discussions which make use of the power of the group to explore the research ideas in depth and in a more diverse way than one to one interviews would allow. The diversity of the group stimulates this intention. There should be six to ten people with two facilitators one of whom asks questions and steers the group discussion; the other acts as a note taker and observer. The focus group is a means to explore an issue, the group members sparking off one another's ideas to develop the collective points of the group. It is important that the facilitator is a strong person able to hold the group's rules and the boundaries of the session. It is important that everyone feels enabled to speak and that the session is not dominated by one or two voices. The purpose of the focus group is to explore a few ideas within the one and a half hours for the session, in depth and to have a diversity of thoughts being shared.

1. Identify the major question for the session.
2. Devise some sub-questions which can be used to guide the discussions between people and support the main question.
3. Develop ground rules *with* the group. Everyone needs to feel able to contribute and to feel respected by their peers.
4. The group needs to work through the questions, remain focused, be polite to one another and to try to get some resolution in its thinking and ideas.
5. The session may be taped or notes taken. It is important to debrief with the fellow facilitator to ensure a shared reading of the event and to have thorough notes of people's ideas and experiences as possible.

Undertaking participatory evaluation with young people

Young people are a particular and often marginalised group because of the ways in which some adults think about and work with young people. There is in some ways a form of 'doublethink' in approaching work with young people. There is a huge volume of programmes and projects created for young people. The evaluations of these projects are often like the programmes themselves, done to young people. Youth are subjects and objects of programmes and of evaluations. Adults gather data and seek to solve youth's problems. This may not be the best approach.

Participatory evaluation with young people is far more enabling of young people and will arguably see a development of better programmes and provisions for young people as the impetus for their development comes from the young people themselves. Just as for adults who become involved in participatory evaluation and become committed to the actions they suggest.

Working with young people through participatory evaluation is a wave gathering more strength as it is seen increasingly as a more sensible way to better understand and support young people's needs and their views of the worlds in which they would like to live. Participatory evaluation is described as 'emerging as a key strategy to achieve the Millennium Development Goals for the year 2015'.[4] Participatory evaluation is also a way in which Articles 12 and 13 of the United Nations Convention on the Rights of the Child[5] can be fulfilled.

Participatory evaluation is a means by which young people can develop a range of skills and interests. They can be are involved in planning and carrying out the evaluation and so become more invested in the findings and developing the programmes which were subject to evaluations. Such programmes could be essential to their particular well-being, for example, those related to good sexual health and avoidance of substance dependency. Young people could be involved in participatory evaluation of key issues facing all ages, like sustainable lifestyles, climate change, provision of welfare and support services. They could be involved in evaluations of community development projects, like planning and the provision of educational services for young people or health services for the community.

The meaning, design, process and methods for undertaking participatory evaluation have been outlined above. Working with young people does not differ in any substantive ways to any of these steps or methods. The purpose continues the same, to 'join together and develop knowledge for action and change'.[6] However, young people and children do differ from adults and some points need to be noted in order to work appropriately and ethically with them.

These include:

- adhering to policies on working with and protecting young people
- understanding that there is a power differential between an adult and a young person and not exploiting this
- ensuring that nothing which is done disadvantages the young person and that all is done for the individual young person's good
- making sure that the training, development and discussion activities are geared to young people. Taking into account their learning styles, youthful energy and interests

As with adults young people may play a variety of roles in participatory evaluation. These may range along a continuum from consultant, exploring youth perspectives and youth issues with adults who initiate evaluations, through to being co-creators of evaluations, to initiating and directing their own evaluations. This latter role involves selection of issue, development of evaluation plan, undertaking data collection and analysis and development of output. Adult expertise may be called upon to support various phases of the work or to help the outputs from the youth initiated evaluation get an audience with adults and decision-makers.

Involving young people in participatory evaluation can have a number of benefits. These can include for young people themselves:

- developing a greater understanding of local realities, possibilities and constraints, which may enhance realistic appreciation of what is possible. These may be viewpoints they share with other young people
- developing other ways of relating to and working with adults
- developing other ways of relating to and working with adults in expert and authority roles
- developing skills and tools for problem solving, analysis and decision-making
- developing a range of research skills
- developing communication, team working and pre-employability skills and experiences
- developing a sense of responsibility towards the project and sense of commitment to carry forward findings
- developing leadership skills and a sense of the power of participatory working for the future

Participatory engagement with young people will improve both the evaluation and the project or programme which is being explored, because young people will bring their perspectives and interests to bear. It will increase appreciation of adult stakeholders of young people's interests and capacities.

Extending participatory monitoring and evaluation into communities' dialogues and development

The final section of this chapter looks very briefly at one element in the development of participatory monitoring and evaluation within an international development context. The reason for this section is to add to an important element into thinking about generating, in an integrated way, dialogue based community development, monitoring and evaluation cycles. Thereby creating a robust cycle of co-learning and co-development which is completely grounded in the needs which are identified by the community. This is a step on from much of the participatory evaluation work which is taking place in the UK, it is a step further towards developing engagement and participation.

Dialogue based social change and development[7] is an iterative series of supported dialogues through which community members define who they are, what they need and how to get what they need in order to improve their own lives. The dialogue is a way to identify problems and envision solutions. The generation of the plans and actions to support the solution creation becomes the community development project. The dialogic process is in itself an evaluatory process; people are assessing what is in place to support them in the future visions which they have for themselves. People are engaged as agents of and for the changes they have co-created for themselves.

The institution of the change structures, which will be a combination of attitudes, ways of doing things, behaviours and resources and their development are supported by what has been described above as participatory monitoring and evaluation. The process of changing is supported by the means to learn about change. The outcomes of participatory evaluation processes drive more change. The process of the evaluation is one of learning about the changes that are taking place.

This integration of the process of instituting change, undertaking change, examining the change and so learning from change in order to further develop and embed beneficial change is the creation of a virtuous and reflective cycle. It requires careful partnership working across local communities and their members, it requires the types of expert support as outlined above. It requires a commitment to work though the difficult processes, including conflicts which come with making changes and working with others. It requires that members of various communities develop new skills and think about their lives in quite other and more empowered ways.

The inclusion of this note about communication for social change should stimulate thinking about more joined up change and evaluation programmes, where there is rooted community ownership.

Summing up

This chapter has taken the commitment of evaluation to learning and change further, by exploring the ways in which stakeholders can become engaged in the evaluation in a variety of roles other than as respondents. It has explored some basic features for participatory evaluation, the emphasis on learning and change oriented outcomes, the emphasis on creative and dialogic evaluation and research methods derived from participatory rural appraisal and the emphasis on community discussions of the emergent findings and issues.

The chapter has considered briefly participatory evaluation with young people and children and closed by suggesting the integration of community developments with participatory evaluation through a more dialogic approach. This is a logical step change in setting up programmes and development work from their outset.

Endnotes

1. IDS (1998) *Participatory Monitoring and Evaluation*. Policy Briefing, Issue 12 www.ids.ac.uk/ids/bookshop/briefs/brief12.html
2. While some participatory evaluation champions may consider learning from mistakes a prerogative of PE there are many evaluators working with other style of evaluation who would also find mistakes or elements which worked less well as a data source to be used.

3. Byrne, A. et al. Eds. (2010) *Measuring Change.* Communication for Social Change Consortium www.communicationforsocialchange.org

4. Gawler, M. (2005) *Useful Tools for Engaging Young People in Participatory Evaluation.* UNICEF.

5. http://www2.ohchr.org/english/law/crc.htm

6. Checkoway, B. and Richards-Schuster, K. *Participatory Evaluation with Young People.* Michigan, University of Michigan.

7. Byrne, A. et al. Eds. (2010) *Measuring Change.* Communication for Social Change Consortium www.communicationforsocialchange.org

10: Working with the Data

Introduction

This chapter moves to some of the final stages of the evaluation, those of working with the accumulated data. It will not have been sensible to collect data without some very clear thoughts as to how to analyse it and the form that the worked up material should take. Indeed the process for analysis of the data should have been part of the plan for data capture, some of the methods of analysis being built into the data collection. For example in writing a questionnaire there will have been a pre-coding of the possible responses ready for their entry into a software package for statistical analysis.

The products from the data collection should have been specified in the contracting process and form part of the contract. There should not be surprises at the close of the work, with the evaluation team being asked to produce other types of report.

In discussing these closing stages it is important to remind ourselves of the utility of the evaluation and its possible roles. It is essential that commissioners and evaluators, having been through the stages of contracting, design and undertaking the evaluation, do not forget that there is still work ahead.

> There is considerable debate between evaluators on such topics as the definition of evaluation, the adoption of experimental and quasi-experimental research designs, and the application of quantitative and qualitative research methods. However there is general consensus that one of the major defining characteristics of evaluation research is that it is intended to be useful.
>
> Clarke, p.173

> Nearly all the literature on evaluation speaks of it as an attempt to serve a decision maker.
> Cronbach, 1982: 5[1]

Possible uses were outlined in the opening chapter; theory-building, knowledge generation, programme improvements, various types of developmental assessments and judgments. The ultimate purpose should have been strongly in the commissioners' sights as they contracted the evaluation and specified its outputs. They still however need to be able to work with those outputs and put them to use. Commissioners are referred back to some of the ground outlined in Chapter 3 on learning and organisations.

This chapter explores some of the closing stages of the evaluation process:

- working with the data
- reporting
- writing recommendations
- sharing the evaluation
- working with the findings
- the feedback loop

Working with the data

The purpose of data analysis is to answer the research questions that guided the evaluation. The data analysis phase should be a bounded task with an end in sight and not be experienced as like being on the back of a runaway horse. Questions may be relatively straight forward, such as:

- has the programme done what it said it was going to do?
- did it do this in the ways in which it intended to?
- with what effects?
- with what impacts?

There are possibilities that the data will yield a number of unanticipated issues, for example negative or positive impacts or consequences of the programme. This is useful data and should be explored, analysed and reported on.

It is possible that the aims of the project cannot be fully commented on because insufficient time has elapsed between for example a group experiencing an intervention and some of the longer-term impacts the project intended. It may be that comment can be made on proxy indicators or interim outcomes that were designed into the evaluation. This should have been discussed earlier on so the evaluator's inability to pass judgment on longer-term impacts should not be a surprise to the commissioners.

Data should be treated with respect. Data should have been collected, labelled and carefully stored until there is readiness to work with it. Once this phase of working with the data begins it should be undertaken in a relatively uninterrupted way. Careful notes should be taken throughout this stage as a means to self-check developing analysis, to record what may seem to be emergent issues and to double check oddities or gaps in the data. Trying to summarise at the close of each day of work what has been noted provides a useful log of working impressions. These can be called upon in report writing, any informal reporting and to self-check.

There are two broad phases in working with the data. The first is the collation of the material; this may be inputting data into a software package, like SPSS[2] or Excel. For qualitative data there will be early processes of identifying and assembling categories of themes and perhaps developing a coding tree. The second phase is that of the data analysis, the exploration of the data, the hunting for patterns and anomalies, the phase of interpretation and drawing conclusions.

There are issues running through all work with data, for example:

- how complete is the data set? For example, the completeness of an interview, the fullness of a survey, the size of the sample compared with the possible sample, whether any groups of stakeholders are missing
- what effect the researcher could exert at this stage to influence the data? Could the researcher exclude data or downplay significance of any data?

It is important that work with the data can be checked for any inputting errors and to re-explore interpretations, to be clear about the size of samples groups and so on.

Qualitative data analysis

This can be approached in a number of ways but the core tasks are similar.

The data falling into the qualitative category could include:

- interview transcripts
- interview notes
- transcripts and notes from focus groups
- observation logs
- participant diaries: written, video or photographic
- participant activities and narratives e.g. tableaux and continua exercises
- participant mapping and photo logs and supporting notes
- the evaluators' field logs

Depending on the size of budget and the scale of the evaluation there may be interview transcripts from one-to-one interviews, group interviews or focus groups. These provide a number of advantages. Firstly, they are a complete record and so should reduce the problems which partial transcription or working from interview notes generates, that of selective focus. Secondly they can help speed up the process of the early work with the data. Provided in digital form the data can be electronically searched for pre-determined coded categories. These materials can be imported into a data analysis package for this process or searched as a word document. The chunks of data with these search words can then be extracted for review. Again this will depend on the sophistication of the project and its budget, the nature of the data and to some extent the straightforwardness of the data. Packages which can be used to work with qualitative data include NVIVO, Nud*ist[3] but they, like any statistical package require training.

Manual analysis of data works in a similar way. Reading through the material several times and looking for patterns, commonalities, anomalies and interesting things, for example, similarities between the data in mentioning certain events or issues, common interpretations and common concerns. If there are respondents who do not conform to these shared understandings what are their understandings? Can categories of issues be created? Are there certain categories with more data in than others? What seems to be of significance in terms of numerical saturation or in ways events or issues are being experienced or interpreted?

Data needs to be reviewed a number of times and ideally by different people to ensure that something obvious or significant has not been overlooked. The process of self-checking is important to ensure that selective reading is not used to confirm in-field hunches. The effects of the relationship between evaluator and commissioners or evaluator and any staff are important. The micro-politics discussed in Chapter 5, can exercise a halo effect and must not interfere with reading the data.

The research questions that have shaped the evaluation will be a framework for exploring the data. The data analysis should be leading to answering those questions.

Quantitative data analysis

The data reviewed could include:

- test scores
- attitude and behaviour surveys
- observations
- questionnaires
- anything with a yes/no, ranked or scalable answers

This involves working with data which mainly already carries a numerical value. For example:

Closed questions

Yes	1
No	2
Don't know	3
No response	9

Make sure to always have a code for this a 'No response'. It is important to know this number as it impacts the response rate for the question and so the significance of the responses to this question.

At the pilot stage this may have shown up something about the way the question was framed which can be followed up.

Licket Scales e.g.

Extremely useful	5
Very useful	4
Reasonably useful	3
A little useful	2
Never found it useful	1
Include a numerical value for the number of times a question was unanswered	e.g. 9

Knowing the number of unanswered questions is important at the analysis stage and may say something about the effectiveness of a question at the pilot stage.

There may be some open-ended questions on a survey or questionnaire where people offer their own responses. This will need to be analysed for any common answers or themes and coded. These categories can be given a numerical value so open-ended questions can be analysed for the frequency of certain types of responses.

The material from open-ended questions can be used for illustrative purposes when writing the report.

The data once extracted from questionnaires and surveys and entered into some type of statistical package can then be analysed, for frequencies, percentages and other descriptive statistics such as medians and modes, and variability of scores. It is important to have training in the use of statistical packages such as SPSS or using Excel if this is a more viable option. It is important to understand what story the data is actually saying otherwise 'It is all too easy to produce impressive-looking nonsense' (Clarke, p.114).

A second caution is that the size of the data pool should always to be noted. 90 per cent looks good, but what does it mean, 90 per cent of 10 people may mean very little and even less if the potential pool of respondents could have been 178. The question is, what about the other 168 potential respondants?

There are a variety of ways in which data may be represented graphically for example, time series, bar charts, scatter diagrams and pie charts. All of which can be easily done with software packages, but it is important to know that what is being represented means something and is not simply an attempt to look smart.

Chapter 1 explored various types of experimental designs and ways to explore causation and distance travelled. It is important to try to triangulate the data to make sure that what looks like a cause, actually is one. Chapter 8 flagged the importance of rules of sample size for various types of analysis. It is important to be trained and to be sure about what it is that is being attempted through statistical reviews of data. Likewise, it is important if trying to make a comparative judgment about a programme or project to have directly comparable data sets. Unless work was framed in this way from the outset it is not likely. Reading evaluation reports of similar types of projects may help provide some contextual grounding and alerts to other possible causative factors or reasons for something. This can be useful, but this is not comparison.

Reporting

Types of report

The traditional form for representing the findings of an evaluation is a final written report. The usual headings including: terms of reference for the evaluation; some history of the programme and organisation which is the subject of the evaluation; other contextual material such as a literature review; outline of the programme or intervention evaluated, its aims and objectives; purpose of the evaluation and its aims; methodology and methodological issues; sample type and size; findings and analysis and a section on recommendations.

There may be a need for several reports for various purposes. These should have been noted in the outputs section of the contract. Typically at the final stage there might be a detailed report for internal use, concentrating on some internal and operational issues that the organisation might not wish to make publically available. There might be a couple of reports for the public domain, for example a summary report for stakeholders and an executive summary for wider sharing.

Interim and progress reporting

There may also have been provision made for interim reports, progress or working papers in addition to final reporting. These earlier reports have several functions, including sharing emergent findings, issues or difficulties. This is important because it may prevent what the commissioners may feel to be unpleasant surprises. It helps if there are difficulties for these to be problem-solved; for example, a particular group of stakeholders being very hard to access.

Early reporting should involve caution, and emergent findings should be carefully flagged as provisional only. It is important that the final report and any recommendations are not rejected because there is a difference of emphasis between an interim report and the final one.

Stakeholders

If there is a range of stakeholders in the audience for the evaluation reports then a range of possible outlets may be explored. Such as:

- project newsletters or entry in organisational or issue-based newsletters
- visual displays: perhaps of work in progress about the evaluation process or about the substantive issues, for example video material or photographs and narratives
- YouTube postings
- web postings
- Facebook updates on the evaluation and inviting responses
- reporting to various audiences
- presentations
- working sessions on the findings

The findings may be shared with a wider audience through local TV and radio interviews, newspapers and at conferences. There will be decisions to make about what elements of the evaluation are presented and this will be the commissioners' call. It is important that those who took part in participatory evaluations are involved in any presentations along with professional evaluators, otherwise there is an untenable disconnect.

Timing

An obvious point but one worth noting; there is no point in a late report or setting the delivery date for a report after the point when decisions should have been made. If there is any risk that a report might be late, the commissioners need to know this and may need some emergent findings to incorporate into their decision-making. Similarly if a report is needed for a particular purpose this should be established when setting the contract and its reporting milestones.

It is important that commissioners wanting to use a report for funding applications are not solely reliant on the report. There may be recommendations for issues which need to be addressed and proper time needs to be allowed for dealing with any such concerns which are raised.

Writing recommendations

Writing recommendations is an element of the report writing process that needs to be taken seriously, although it is not a feature of all evaluations.

The interpretation and analysis of data and the conclusions drawn are facts and this work should be open to checking for accuracy. Making recommendations can be somewhat more creative: they are the evaluators' suggestions and should not be mixed in with other sections of the report, in the conclusions, for example.

Recommendations should be considered carefully. They should flow from issues identified through the data analysis and should be embedded in matters raised in the conclusions. Recommendations should be adoptable and resonate with the evaluation report and the organisation. Outlandish recommendations, those that are context-free or those simply courting further research work with will probably make little sense and will not be adoptable. It is important though that recommendations offer some fresh thinking.

Recommendations should be organised according to what element of the work is being targeted. They should express the suggestion simply and then sketch it out in full. There should be a section reviewing possible implications of each recommendation both positive and negative. These might include for example, re-rolling existing resources, initial cost implications, savings, efficiencies, greater take-up of services, redundancies and their associated costs, development of new policies or staff training. Wherever possible model these recommendations with actual existing data on costs, staffing or service take-up. If there is no existing data then a best estimate should be developed.

A sense of the timescale for each recommendation should be included. It needs to be noted whether one recommendation is contingent upon another or if there is any sequencing to the recommendations. The recommendations should also indicate clearly if it is the responsibility of a certain stakeholder group or functional role. Presentation of the recommendations should be made in full. A summary in matrix form may also be helpful.

Recommendations may impact policy development, use and allocation of resources, staffing ratios and types, staff development, operational standards, the closure of lines of service and the expansion of lines of service. Depending on the extent of the evaluation findings and recommendations they can impact business and strategic planning, staff development and appraisal cycles.

It is the responsibility of the evaluation team to try to think through the ramifications of the recommendations they propose and to present these. However, the evaluation team is not running the organisation or programme and is not going to be: it should have no more than dispassionate interest in the suggestions it offers up.

It is important that the evaluators and the organisation are aware of the boundaries of the evaluator role unless role extensions have been previously agreed when both groups should be mindful of issues

Recommendation	Target area	Intended improvement or development	Intended benefits e.g. efficiencies savings	Dis-benefits	Responsibility to carry forward	Financial and other costs	Impacts to: policy, staff, costs, stakeholders, service users, current accommodation	Timescale

Diagram 21: Recommendations matrix

arising from this. If the evaluation was undertaken as a developmental evaluation the evaluators are still in the roles of helping decision making through the use of their analysis and cultivating the skills of analysis and evaluative thinking in the decision-makers.

Sharing the evaluation

Evaluation is a process of judging. The evaluation can come at many stages of an organisation's work: allied to the very early processes of needs analysis, during the process of service delivery, as a formative evaluation. It might concentrate on operational processes and be geared to their improvement or it may focus on intervention impacts. Whatever the purpose of the evaluation it should be more than just a filed report.

Thought should be given to sharing the report. This may be for a number of reasons, not least of all those driven by concern about power, values and fairness:

- those who participated in the evaluation have given their time, and sharing a report with them acknowledges the investment of their time and their interest in the work
- in sharing the report make it clear what was reported, the interpretations of the data, the conclusions and recommendations. If there has been no sharing of this material while the evaluation was in progress then sharing at this stage allows for some come-back and checking. It allows people to have some sense of recourse if they feel that the work was inaccurate. A mechanism for collecting feedback would have to be developed and a mechanism created for dealing with opinions expressed or concerns raised. There is no point in asking for feedback and then not using it
- sharing the report allays any concerns about any misrepresentations. That some stakeholders may have been blamed, that there may be criticisms of staff groups or that there may have been breaches of confidentiality

Aside from dealing with these types of concerns sharing the report amongst stakeholders is an opportunity for using this as a data phase and developmental phase in its own right. The report could be shared for example with a variety of the stakeholder groups. These might include:

- trustees
- senior managers
- staff of all levels and types
- users of services
- other organisations
- umbrella and membership organisations to which the organisation commissioning the evaluation belongs
- funders of the organisation
- regional or local policy makers which are interested in or have responsibilities for the area of work of the evaluated organisation
- general public

This process would allow some of the issues and ideas in the report to be viewed through very different perspectives and very different types of creativity could be brought to the table. Wider groups could be involved in thinking about taking forward any recommendations and how to do so.

The findings may be valuable for local policy development, to support development work or to add to the knowledge of an umbrella or membership organisation when the work may be useful for organisations wrestling with similar issues.

Working with the findings

This can be a hard phase for some of the stakeholders. For example:

- there may be difficulties for a board or senior management group in looking at shortfalls in the organisation. It may seem to them to be too overwhelming to do anything. This may be because the organisation has not been reviewing its programmes or service for some time and they now seem lacklustre or not to be meeting needs or the external environment may have changed. The organisation may not have the internal capacity or will to make changes
- there may be a lack of perspective in seeing any problems because the collective commitment is so great to what is being done that there is a refusal to see that any provision or personnel warrants an overhaul
- there may be factions in the management team or the board and the evaluation findings may play to those divisions. Disagreements over the problems and solutions may take up the time as opposed to working on a strategy to make use of the findings
- there may be disappointment in the findings because the expectations for the evaluation have not been realised
- the evaluation may have been intended as symbolic as opposed being utilised

These are difficulties and there may be criticisms of the evaluation as a way of deflecting from actually having to take note of the contents of the report and the recommendations. Chapter 3 explored some of the issues which organisations may have in admitting the perspectives of others external to the organisation.

The report and recommendations may be well received but the organisation may not know what to do and may expect the evaluators to continue to take the work forward. This can become problematic. For example:

- if the evaluators become involved in trying to carry forward their recommendations how vested will they become in their recommendations and how much will they be able to work with other suggestions which may better meet the needs of stakeholders?
- if the evaluators take on a developmental role who will undertake subsequent evaluations? The initial evaluators will be too vested to do so: but they will have had the baseline knowledge about the programme or organisation which is something new evaluators would have to try to retrospectively reconstruct

Suggestions for taking forward recommendations were explored in Chapter 3 and could include:

- away days and organisational retreats to focus on parts of the evaluation and recommendations
- staff training commissioned to meet areas of short-fall
- working groups to take elements of the report
- action research groups to focus on the development of recommendations
- cross stakeholder working groups to get diversity of opinions and ideas
- ruthless prioritising of issues and recommendations to dovetail with business and strategic planning processes
- adopting a few recommendations and issues and using these in planning staff development and annual appraisal
- reviewing existing monitoring and internal review arrangements to align with evaluation issues and adopt some similar categories of analysis in the evaluation report to show progress on identified issues

There will need to be an acknowledgement of the role that resistance to change can play in trying to ignore recommendations or the issues that were highlighted by the evaluation. There will need to be acknowledgement of the practicalities of organisational operation such as:

- funding and time which will be required to explore and implement changes
- the imperatives to continue day to day work
- the pressures of funding cycles
- the restrictions and goals of funders

The feedback loop

In the end the worth of evaluations must be judged by their utility.

Rossi and Freeman, 1993: 443[4]

There are three elements to explore in this section:

- what is the stakeholders' evaluation of the outputs and process of the evaluation experience?
- how are the evaluation reports and recommendations being taken forward?
- what have the stakeholders learned?

Firstly it is important that the evaluator and team know if the ways in which they have worked, the data collected, analysed and the reporting have been of use to the various stakeholders. It is good practice to review the evaluation process and the outputs as this is an opportunity for the evaluation team to learn about its own processes and impacts. It is also an opportunity for the stakeholders to think about the process they have experienced and how this may contribute to their learning about approaching subsequent evaluations. There may be some risk in this to the evaluators' feelings if the process or products have been a disappointment but it is likely that this will already have been made clear. Trying to tease out why this is so may help in approaching future work.

Secondly once the evaluators complete their, and there is often little follow up and little feedback about whether their findings have been useful or not. Knowledge of what may be happening with the work helps the evaluator develop greater competence in writing recommendations and it helps remind the stakeholders that one of the roles of evaluative reporting is to help them in their work.

A final reason for asking for reflection on the evaluation is to help the stakeholders examine their own role in commissioning and working with an evaluation. While it is easy to shift the blame onto the evaluators if they have produced a report which is not liked it is important for those who commissioned the work to think about their own role. Were they trying to buy a certain view or endorsement of their own ideas? Was access prevented for data collection? Were the objectives of project or evaluation too vague? Is there resistance to hearing that something was less successful than they had hoped?

A schedule could be devised using some of the following headings and questions:

Overall – knowledge and utility

How has knowledge or understanding been extended by the evaluation?

In what ways?

How might this knowledge be used?

How has the evaluation been useful?

How useful have the recommendations been?

What else might have been done to improve the recommendations?

How has the evaluation been used to take the organisation's work forward?

How is it envisaged that the evaluation can be used to take the organisation's work forward?

What else is needed to take the organisation's work forward?

Overall – your learning

What has been learnt from the evaluation process? Consider the stages of the work from discussing objectives through to receiving the report

What else might the organisation have done to better support the evaluation?

What more could the evaluation team have done to help the organisation understand the evaluation process?

What more could the evaluation have done to help the organisation's learning?

What has been learnt about evaluation?

Is there anything that the organisation will take from this work to incorporate into its own monitoring or evaluation?

Thoroughness and diversity

How well has the evaluation addressed the organisation's aims and objectives?

Do you have a sense that the organisation has been thoroughly explored?

Do you feel the richness of the organisation has been explored in the evaluation report?

Where do you feel there may be gaps? How important is this to you?

Did the evaluation explore diverse perspectives?

How well did the analysis and reporting represent such diversity of perspectives?

Do you feel the conclusions and recommendations are well grounded in an experience of the organisation's work?

Weaknesses

In what ways, if at all, did the evaluation not meet expectations?

Are there any concerns about any ethical issues?

Are there any concerns about the conduct of the fieldwork?

Are there any concerns that any perspective has not been given due consideration?

Are there any concerns that there is something missing in the reporting?

Please make comments on any areas that these questions have not covered.

Seeking such feedback helps in the generation of double loop if not triple loop learning for all concerned. It is important to continue to question assumptions about knowledge and its development and not to see the end of the evaluation as a terminal stage and to let a project languish there.

Summing up

This chapter has explored the closing stages of the evaluation. It is important that interest and commitment do not flag in these final stages. No matter what struggles there may have been in getting the evaluation underway and undertaking the data collection, if due attention is not paid at this stage all that effort will have been pointless.

This obligation extends to those commissioning the evaluation as well as the evaluation team. The report will only have value if it is useful and it will only be useful if the project team or commissioners make some use of the knowledge, conclusions and, if provided, recommendations.

Taking some time to complete the process by soliciting feedback on the evaluation and its outputs will be helpful to the evaluation team, to those commissioning the work and to those being evaluated. Trying to make sense at this stage will reinforce and enrich the learning.

Endnotes

1. Clarke, A. (1999) *Evaluation Research*, London, Sage. Cronbach, L.J. (1982) *Designing Evaluations of Educational and Social Programs*. San Francisco, Jossey Bass.
2. Statistical Package for the Social Sciences.
3. Two examples of qualitative data review packages. There are others.
4. Rossi, P. and Freeman, H.E. (1993) *Evaluation: A Systematic Approach*. London, Sage.

11: Managing Feelings in the Field

Introduction

The human element in the evaluation process has been a theme throughout the book and this chapter offers some further reflections on this. Evaluations seem risky: they expose an organisation to having to think about itself and to perhaps unpick some of those defences explored in Chapter 3. Evaluations mean people outside the organisation or programme make judgments about it. Participatory evaluations help people learn, develop new skills, work and interact with others in ways which they have not previously done, which can be alarming as well as exhilarating.

It is not surprising that somewhere along the line in any evaluation there will be people who feel stressed by, or become less committed to, the evaluation. This chapter explores some of the ways in which feelings may affect an evaluation. Discussion of emotions and feelings are not commonly found in the literature on research and evaluation and yet they are a crucial element. For evaluators the ground explored in this chapter is the type of data that should be included in the Evaluation Log. For commissioners and others it is helpful to have awareness and insight into the role emotions may play, to be aware they can be common experiences and to be alive to what is actually going on and not allow feelings to stall an evaluation.

The evaluated

As a starting point here are two exercises that may prove useful.

Images and associations

Individually, consider the word evaluation and list the images, ideas and associations that come to mind. It is more worthwhile to get the volume of ideas rather than work up any single one completely.

Share these ideas with a group of colleagues and explore: Are there any commonalities across the group? Are there any questions which emerge from these lists of ideas? Are there any actions which might be taken? What can be shared with evaluators?

Hopes, concerns and fears

An exercise often presented at the beginning of courses and events is that of listing hopes, expectations and fears. It is worth undertaking at the outset of an evaluation to see what emerges for individuals and if there are any patterns across groups.

For example, particular groups of staff may be concerned about blame; there may be functions within an organisation concerned about what might be said; for example, that leadership may be lacking. While this is a hard exercise it is a useful piece of reflective work to undertake to surface issues, to share concerns with the evaluation team and to begin to highlight elements of work an organisation needs to do and for which it may need some external help.

It might be useful to check periodically if any negative feelings, projections or unreasonable expectations continue to play themselves out in the back of people's minds as an evaluation proceeds.

As was explored in Chapter 3 organisations through their members develop a particular sense of purpose and identity, individuals in those organisations become very aligned with the organisations they work for, often investing much of their sense of self and well-being in such organisations. The relationship, almost symbiotic, can become threatened by an evaluation. The evaluator can present as a challenge: asking questions and trying to exhume evidence to support various statements about for example, benefits, competence and success. The sense of challenge may be especially strong with smaller or self-styled alternative organisations who are dependent on regular increments of funding to keep their work going. The evaluation and its findings may well be tied to this funding.

The evaluation can inadvertently break down organisational defences and draw internal conflicts towards itself: the evaluation can become a vehicle to carry the conflicts the group does not want to express. Evaluation may raise doubts, which otherwise would be suppressed about other internal and external groups. Little about the ways in which evaluators conduct their work will stem such feelings.

Organisations may do well to decide how their agency can work with an evaluation as opposed to feeling passive or being threatened by it.

The evaluator and team

Field relationships exercise

An exercise that may prove useful for the evaluation team is that of drawing out the relationships between the team and various stakeholder groups or individual stakeholders (see Diagram 22). The circles represent different stakeholder groups, they may be closer or further from the evaluation team and the differences in sizes represent the differences in perceived importance. The circles can be joined to the team with lines to show the strength of the relationship. Arrows added to the lines can show the direction of communications which may be one or two way.

Finally lines and arrows of communication can be drawn between the stakeholder circles to show relationship and influence between the stakeholder groups.

The analysis of what has been depicted may show interfaces such as:

- undue influence given to certain stakeholder groups
- that some stakeholder groups are missing from the depiction
- that there is a strong relationship or more two-way communication with some groups than others

This exercise may be done by individual team members and the results then compared across the team. This can be undertaken as a group exercise, keeping note of points raised in the discussions.

It will be for each team to determine if the balances in relationships are right, if there are some balances and lines of communication which may exert an unfortunate effect and if there is any rebalancing to be done. The exercise may give clues as to why field relationships are developing in certain ways?

It might be useful to repeat this exercise periodically.

Emotion may affect the contractor-evaluator relationship in many ways. Emotions coming from the contractor and the organisation could include:

- resentments at having been forced to have the evaluation and some control of access to data
- trying to play the evaluation team by only allowing access to certain data

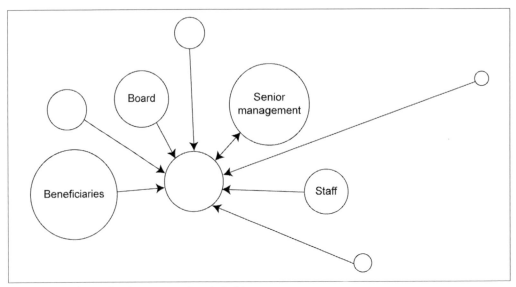

Diagram 22: The evaluation team and stakeholders

- defensiveness
- trying to use the evaluation, to breech the boundaries of confidentiality and prize from the researcher privileged information about activities and staff
- placing undue pressure on the evaluation to report only on certain elements of the work
- neutrality and a business-like approach to the evaluation
- disappointment at the evaluation outcomes
- trying make the evaluation team party to the organisation's problems or issues, for example with funding and trying to place a burden of responsibility or guilt on the evaluation team to report only the positive
- huge enthusiasm for the evaluation and making access to data easy

Some feelings may get in the way of conducting the evaluation and in some instances these will need to be attended to in order that the fieldwork may continue. For example, access to data may be frustrated, support for the evaluation may evaporate, there may be pressures to report earlier than agreed in the contract or findings may be disputed. The contract may need to be invoked formally or informally as it is a touchstone of a time when there was agreement and the symbolic value of this may need to be reinforced.

It is important for the team to record feelings and emotional experiences in play in order to try to make sense of what is going on, to maintain some distance and perspective and to think how best to develop a strategy. It will be useful to see if less helpful emotions come from only certain stakeholders or individuals and to try to decide why this may be so.

The evaluator cannot necessarily re-channel the feelings that the evaluation is stirring up but trying to keep the flow of communication going as appropriate with senior managers and stakeholders may help. There should be reporting points in the contract, which should be adhered to and any issues challenging the evaluation emerging from the data as significant, should be highlighted.

A sort of cold conflict can develop and stall the evaluation.[1] In the face of criticism or adverse comments it is important to try to get at what it is that is wrong. The following points may help:

- don't flannel or cover over problems, inauthenticity will be obvious

- offer to investigate and get to the bottom of concerns and complaints
- present possible solutions to issues
- if there are misconceptions work to try to explore these and to correct them – the contract, if not used heavy-handedly will help, make use of others who can support the contractor–evaluator relationship in these conversations
- not blaming, lying or scapegoating on your part may help de-escalate any tendency on the part of the contractor
- offering to re-work something or to make some other sort of concession so long as this is going to be effective and is not succumbing to bullying may be helpful and smooth the way. It should not be done if this is then going to become a precedent[2]

Support for the evaluation team

Line management or supervisory support for the lead evaluator

The evaluator will need to make use of support and line management to explore problematic areas and develop perspectives and strategies. Pressures in some evaluation situations can be great and it is important to maintain a level head in order to continue to make appropriately professional decisions.

External evaluators

Line management or supervision is a potential source of helpful insight for substantive, contractual and emotional material generated in an evaluation. There is a need for effective supervision and a safe place for recourse for help. Difficulties should be flagged with the line manager. It is important that, as soon as issues emerge, they are explored, otherwise it is likely that problems could become bigger.

If the external evaluator is without a line manager there should be some arrangement for a supervisor to be in place to help support the maintenance of perspective and problem resolution.

Internal evaluators

This is potentially a most complex relationship and may generate a number of conflicting feelings. Some supervisory support or an external consultant to offer support is important. It may be hard for the internal evaluator to flag concerns and issues with their line manager. They may feel compelled to play down issues in case they are seen as a sign of their own competence.

For the internal evaluator there can be problems in trying to gather data from colleagues, in asking for privileged information and interviewing superiors. The evaluator may feel pressure to find and report only positives, and have a sense of being a betrayer if this cannot be done.

The evaluation team

The evaluation team, like any other, requires management with sensitivity, support, clarity and feedback. While there may be many external distractions in getting an evaluation underway, working in a new area, making new relationships with stakeholders and cultivating the relationship with the commissioning body it is important not to lose focus on the relationships within the team. It may be that the team has worked together extensively before, or it may have been pulled together for a specific assignment. It may be that the team has a number of interns or that there is a participatory element to the evaluation.

All relationships with team members require attention, management and importantly not making assumptions. There may be buddying and teaching roles to play with less experienced team members. Responsibilities with accountability and resources should be allocated for doing this.

Key elements to make the work run more effectively could include:

- very full initial briefings about the substantive area, methodology, design and research tools
- working through the research tools with team members so they understand what is being sought and how the tools work
- briefing about the contract and contractual issues impacting the team's work. Being clear about any particular expectations from the contracting organisation or any key policies
- having contact and emergency information and procedures for researcher safety in place. Making sure there are protocols for working in the field and that less experienced researchers are well aware of these
- researchers may need to know how to handle respondents who become upset or how to signpost respondents for help. It is important to know the line between research and counselling, research and befriending and the limitations of the roles to be played in the field. This is especially important where there is face-to-face data collection, use of psycho-social methods, where there are less experienced researchers or experienced researchers who are beginning to take things for granted and where the material is difficult
- opportunities need to be provided for researchers to seek debriefing if they are impacted adversely by anything
- supervision sessions need to be timetabled to explore any issues emerging in the field and in field relationships
- there should be a clear cycle of team meetings with changing expectations to reflect the changing life cycle of the evaluation
- make no assumptions and check early on the quality of data collection, level of insight and analysis amongst different team members

The impact of fieldwork

Qualitative research has particular demands. The researcher is using much of themselves as a tool to establish rapport, to be sensitive to field issues and to work through whatever is needed to collect the data. This can sometimes be lonely, demanding and unsatisfying. It is important that research team members have support from each other and the evaluation leader.

There may be ways in which various personal characteristics of research team members impact interactions in the field. These are not things about which anything can be done, other than to understand them for what they are and consider the data value of the experience. There is for example documentation about the ways gender affects the perceptions of a researcher, the researcher being assigned social roles which are more comfortable to the respondent. Warren writes of the ways in which her status as a professor and researcher was changed:

> In the mental health court I studied for example where young women were typically either law students or assistants or visiting nursing students, I was treated as one or another of these social types . . . in the mental hospitals I visited . . . despite my introduction . . . I was taken for a visiting student, usually a nursing student.[3]

The management of personal boundaries becomes important in trying not to become absorbed into anyone else's construction of who the researcher is supposed to be or what they are doing. It is important that the researcher does not become confused about their own role, and does not become exhausted by adopting multiple roles in the field.[4]

The evaluator may take on multiple projections from different people. These may not surface until the evaluation moves closer to the actual data collection. This can be confusing for the evaluator and those evaluated who may experience a shift from being okay about the evaluator and the evaluation to feeling bothered or threatened or not wanting someone poking about in their work. People have multiple feelings towards authority and the evaluator can become a representative of that broad category of authority. Defensiveness, ambivalence, fear of self-disclosure, desire to self-disclose or to seek help may bounce about in the various reactions and interactions with the evaluator. It is important to try to untangle these responses, to encourage a joint focus on the task and not to allow feelings to drift. Evaluative judgments made by people who are more responsive make the work easier, more enjoyable and the data more accessible.

The emotions around reporting

At the closing stages of the work emotions may surface. After withdrawing from the field the evaluation team may shrink to one or two people who are tasked to work on data analysis and report writing. This can be a lonely stage and one beset with doubts. There may have been pressures to present only certain facts, there may be concerns that less favourable findings will lead to disputes, there may be concerns about the writing process or there may be issues with the work flow with the demands of other contracts starting as one is closing.

In handing over the report there may be disappointments in store for the evaluator and team. Firstly a report may not be acknowledged for the amount of work that has been undertaken, the quality of the findings and recommendation. It may be discounted and disputed. This can lead to repercussions, with some stakeholders feeling betrayed if after giving their time to the evaluation there is no discussion of the report and nothing is put in motion to generate change. The evaluation team can feel like organisational scapegoats. It is important to try to encourage the commissioners to not shoot the messenger. This may not be possible and this may be a response that the team has to live with.

For evaluations involving policy as opposed to organisation, it may be that the findings and analysis, however well grounded, cannot compete with the pressures of a policy agenda. The evaluation is in effect ignored, as findings may not accord with the ways policy is being framed and rolled out.

At worst, a commissioning body may want to dispute the report and possibly not honour their side of the contract. Costs will have been incurred and there will be a risk to the evaluation team's reputation. Ways forward will need to be found to resolve the situation without compromising integrity. Needless to say if a bad job, for whatever reason, has been done then this will need to be put right. It is important to be mindful of the fact that the research site should not be spoiled for others. If there is a difference of opinion over the findings and their interpretation strategies which might be employed:

- soul search and re-check the data set to see if the team's ideas stand up to further scrutiny
- ask another evaluator colleague to look at the site, the data and the report and see what conclusions they come to
- see if the report can be shared more widely with stakeholders to see if it resonates with them
- find some way to explore the points of difference and then either one side or the other may change its mind, if not then incorporate the discussion into the report in some form

Summing up

Evaluation is a human enterprise and one where people feel a sense of risk. It is important to be mindful of this at all stages of the evaluation process. It is possible that evaluation teams will have to manage less positive responses to their work. Reflection and analysis applied to these issues will help, as will frequent team communications and meetings and supervision. The chapter has offered some suggestions for ways to think about how to head off situations at the pass as opposed to allowing them to develop.

Endnotes

1. Fritchie, R. and Leary, M. (1998) *Resolving Conflicts in Organisations.* London, Lemos and Crane.
2. See also Heerkins, G. (2002) *Project Management.* New York, McGraw Hill.
3. Warren, C. (1988) *Gender Issues in Field Research.* California, Sage.
4. Squirrell, G. (1993) *Like Zulus Against the Gattling Gun.* PhD thesis, University of Bristol.

Concluding Comments

This is not the last book you will read on evaluation as you develop your practice. At a number of points in the text it is suggested there are areas to explore in more depth, for example organisational learning, certain research methods and the range of possible methodologies. This discussion of evaluation has tried to combine a number of elements to stimulate your thinking, to inform your practice of evaluation if you are an evaluator; to inform the framing and conceptualisation of the role and uses of evaluation if you commission evaluations. Several themes have been highlighted throughout the book and so to briefly recapitulate:

Evaluation is a matter of choices not of slavish devotion to one methodology or framework. There are choices to be made depending on the purpose of the work and its uses. There may be ways to work with evaluation not hitherto considered, for example, democratic and developmental evaluation.

Evaluation can be undertaken in ways which are inclusive, which encourage and enable the development of voice and articulation of opinions from various communities. It can support opinion-sharing across communities and the development of shared understandings. It can support the development of democratic decision-making. Participatory evaluations can develop a range of skills and attitudes, including communication, leadership, evaluative and critical thinking skills.

Evaluations can be creative processes and creative in their outcomes. They can be undertaken in ways that drive members of different communities to work together to forge a strategy for the evaluation and to work together to undertake it. Participatorily created evaluations drawing on expert support may combine very different insights into issues and ways of working to create completely new frames of reference, some explanations of issues and innovative solutions.

Evaluations may be devised in ways which generate opportunities for many stakeholders to be involved in contributing to data sets, through a multitude of ways to capture data; for example, making video recordings, taking photographs, story telling and social mapping. They can enable the fusion of different points of view and the generation of creative and consensus understandings. They can be undertaken using a range of interesting methods that capture imaginations and develop the skills of those engaged in them.

Evaluation is a source of learning. It is an activity that can be co-operative and can encourage the development of skills. Its processes offer opportunities to reflect on what is being done through the learning opportunities generated by the arrival of outsiders into the organisational boundary. Evaluative outputs are occasions for organisations, for example, developers of interventions to think critically about what is being done, to learn from the mirror which is held up to them and to drive their reflections based on the evaluative considerations of others.

Evaluation can be a radical way of working. Developmental evaluation works with social innovations and entrepreneurs who are forging new ways of working with complex social problems. It provides in real-time grounded analysis of the ways in which problems are conceptualised and of the solutions being developed. It provides material which can be used by decision makers, in the here and now, to revise and move on what they are doing. Developmental evaluation makes the bridge between working as an evaluator and as an organisational consultant, allowing evaluative expertise and critical thinking to inform the learning processes of organisations.

Evaluation stimulates and supports learning. There has been an emphasis in the book on evaluation as a means to promote learning by drawing from what is actually presented as opposed to conceptualising evaluation as being used to support what is known. Evaluation should be considered as part of an organisation's learning cycle and ways should be created to work with its findings, to use the findings to stimulate developments through more creative and colleagial means, such as communities of practice and Action Learning.

Throughout the text the *humanity of the enterprise* has been emphasised. People's sense of self and well-being is tied into their work and their communities. The arrival of an evaluation is significant, and it can be a fearful disturbance into an existing situation, which whether or not the situation is optimal is a known one. There has been emphasis placed on the role of the commissioners to think carefully about the purpose of the evaluation and how it might be used. The importance of contracting, of adopting others' perspectives and of thinking carefully ahead of time has been emphasised. The role of the evaluators, the importance of supervision and support for them to help maintain focus and the emphasis on communication has been stressed. Working with emergence and accommodating emergence within the evaluation plan keeps the project human.

Paying attention to ethics, politics, multiple perspectives, values and realities have run as core themes throughout the book. Evaluation is a lot about choices and about cultivating an evaluative way of thinking and analysing.

Suggestions for Exploration

In thinking about developing your own reading in the areas covered by this book full use should be made of the endnotes. In addition there are some references below for key organisations in the field and some suggestions for readings in areas that extend what it has been possible to cover in this book.

The field is broad and not everything can be referenced in the endnotes or in this short suggestions list: omissions are not meant to be disrespectful or disregarding of good work.

Evaluation

Fetterman, D. (2004) *Empowerment Evaluation Principles in Practice*, Surrey, Guilford Press.
Mertens, D. (2008) *Transformative Research and Evaluation*, Surrey, Guilford Press.
Patton, (2008) *Utilisation-Focused Evaluation.* 4th edn London, Sage.
Patton, M. (2001) *Qualitative Research and Evaluation Methods.* 3rd edn. London, Sage.
Weiss, C. (1997) *Evaluation.* 2nd edn. London, Prentice Hall.

Research methods and data analysis

Broussine, M. (Ed.) (2008) *Creative Methods in Organisational Research.* London, Sage.
Bryman, A. (2001) *Social Research Methods.* Oxford, Oxford University Press.
Denzin, N. and Lincoln, Y. (Eds.) (2003) *Strategies of Qualitative Enquiry.* 2nd edn. London, Sage.
Gilbert, N. (Ed.) (2001) *Researching Social Life.* 2nd edn. London, Sage.
Keats, D. (2000) *Interviewing.* Milton Keynes, Open University Press.
Punch, K. (2001) *Introduction to Social Research.* London, Sage.
Rubin, H. and Rubin, I. (1995) *Qualitative Interviewing: The Art of Hearing Data.* London, Sage.
Sapsford, R. and Jupp, V. (1996) *Data Collection and Analysis.* London, Sage.
Silverman, D. (2001) *Interpreting Qualitative Data.* 2nd edn. London, Sage.
Silverman, D. (2000) *Doing Qualitative Research.* London, Sage.
Wolcott, H. (1995) *The Art of Fieldwork.* Walnut Creek, Alta Mira.

Organisations working with learning and change

Argyris, C. (1999) *On Organisational Learning.* London, Blackwell.
Brown, A. (1998) *Organisational Culture.* London, Pitman.
Fineman, S. et al. (2005) *Organising and Organisations.* London, Sage.
Mabey, C. and Iles, (Eds.) (1994) *Managing Learning.* London, Routledge.
McGill, I. and Beaty, L. (2002) *Action Learning.* 2nd edn. London, Routledge.
McGill, I. and Brockbank, A. (2004) *The Action Learning Handbook.* London, Routledge.
Oliver, C. (2005) *Reflexive Enquiry.* London, Karnac Books.
Pedler, M. et al. (1997) *The Learning Company.* 2nd edn. London, McGraw Hill.
Senge, M. et al. (1999) *The Dance of Change.* London, Nicholas Brealey.

Really useful organisations for evaluation, social policy and community engagement

Aspen Institute http://www.aspeninstitute.org
Barnados http://www.barnardos.org.uk

Charities Evaluation Service http://www.ces-vol.org.uk
Demos http://www.demos.co.uk
Involve http://www.involve.org.uk
Joseph Rowntree http://www.jrf.org.uk
National Council for Voluntary Organisations http://www.ncvo-vol.org.uk
NESTA http://www.nesta.org.uk
New Economics Foundation http://www.neweconomics.org
Research Development and Statistics, Home Office http://rds.homeoffice.gov.uk/rds
Social Science Research Update, University of Surrey http://sru.soc.surrey.ac.uk
UNICEFhttp://www.unicef.org
United Kingdom Evaluation Society http://www.evaluation.org.uk

Becoming an effective trainer
By Gillian Squirrell

'Particularly valuable . . . It is presented accessibly and balances theory and practice.' Community Care

'An ongoing source of reference and help.' Youthwork.

'Promotes all the right messages.' www.trainingzone.co.uk.

978-1-898924-26-5

Inter-agency training
A practical handbook
By Jo Edwards and Ane Freed-Kernis

Using the example of Local Safeguarding Children Boards, but adaptable for different circumstances and disciplines, the guidance and tools in this handbook will help ensure that inter-agency training happens, is of good quality, and enhances inter-agency communication and cooperation. It aims to empower and develop resilience. Practical in focus, with underlying theory offered where useful, and extensively tried and tested, it offers: tools, exercises and checklists for use at each stage of the training cycle – from planning to evaluation; strategies for when you encounter obstacles; an opportunity to appraise, affirm and develop trainers' own skills and knowledge; inspiration to try something new and different.

978-1-905541-72-0

Engagement in practice
Theory and practice for successful engagement
By Gillian Squirrell

That engagement and participation have been concepts and practices which have been advanced and supported by governments of different political persuasions signals how much engagement matters. It is as important for voluntary, community, not-for-profit and private organisations as it is for all types of public services and for all levels of government.

It can and should be a transformative way of working, developing insights and deepening relationships between communities; but sometimes it can lead people — particularly those already disempowered — to feel further excluded, unheard, or betrayed.

Engagement in Practice is useful to those:

- commissioning, orchestrating, instigating or evaluating engagement work
- involved in engagement, as stakeholders, at any level - including professionals, facilitators. people in community organisations, citizens.

It is also invaluable for students, lecturers and researchers, and libraries that serve them.

The book urges readers to reflect critically how engagement practice can involve making informed ethical decisions, being appreciative of others, and being aware of the impacts of what is done on reinforcing or challenging the existing status quo.

Supporting resources are available on-line at www.e2rc.net.

978-1-905541-75-1

Developing life skills
By Gillian Squirrell

'The sheer amount of good material makes it a worthwhile purchase . . . It's good on getting people to relate their thinking to their own life, rather than just keeping it at a distance.' Youthwork.

'Based on the conviction that adults, as well as young people, continue to learn, change and develop throughout their lives, and that life skills can be learned . . . it provides everything a trainer might need to construct a learning programme.' Vista.

978-1-898924-27-2

Developing social skills
By Gillian Squirrell

'An invaluable tool . . . a set of accessible and systematic materials that can be used straight off the shelf . . . it is all there in the one tome.' Youth and Policy.

'Suitable for participants with a range of abilities . . . this is a useful and well written manual.' PSW.

978-1-898924-28-9

Leadership
Being effective and remaining human
By Peter Gilbert

'Asserts a powerful and clear image of the human service leader.' The International Journal of Leadership in Public Service.

'The chapter on the use – and potential abuse – of personal power and authority is essential reading . . . suitable for anyone practising leadership at whatever level and provides excellent scope for reflection on personal aspirations and performance.' Social Caring.

978-1-903855-76-8

Power and empowerment
By Neil Thompson

'An altogether more subtle and compelling analysis . . . I can see experienced practitioners and practice teachers enjoying it. This is a book that goes well beyond the rhetoric.' Professor Mark Doel, Sheffield Hallam University.

978-1-903855-99-7

Partnership made painless
A joined-up guide to working together
By Ros Harrison, Geoffrey Mann, Michael Murphy, Alan Taylor and Neil Thompson

'Until now there has been no book that sought to give practitioners or managers explicit guidance in how to make partnerships work. This volume seeks to fill that gap . . . it does so admirably . . . an accessible 'how-to-do-it' approach . . . the practical experience of the authors in establishing and nurturing partnerships does give the book the feel of lived reality . . . clear and succinct.' Vista.

'How refreshing to read a book that goes beyond the rhetoric and addresses some of the problems which can accompany it . . . will be of practical help.' Community Care.

978-1-898924-88-3